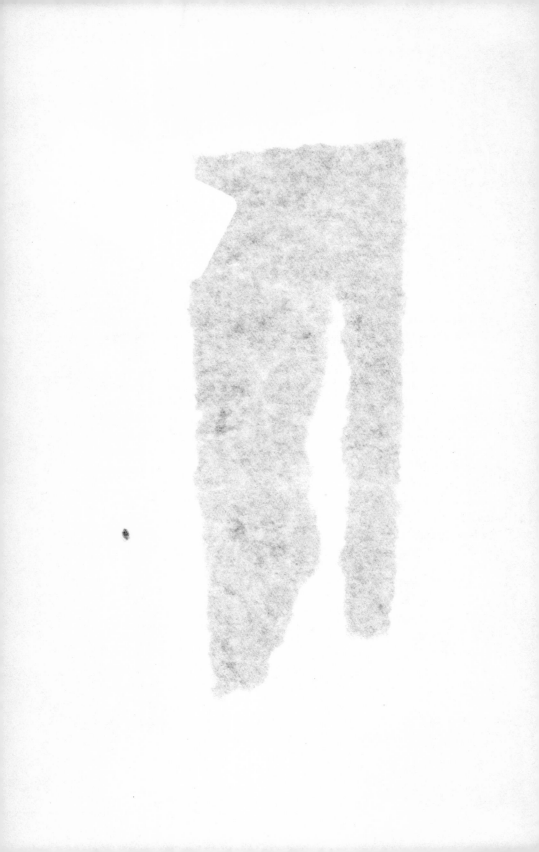

MAN AND ANIMALS

ABOUT THE BOOK

Elephant and pig, dog and goose, horse and silkworm, cat and sheep, quail and mink have lived inside human communities since civilisation began. In fact, civilisation as we know it would have been inconceivable without the horse, the cow, the sheep, and in other parts of the world without reindeer or dog or the llama.

In fascinating and tender detail, Barloy traces the growth of man's interdependence with domesticated animals. The Egyptians trained the North African cat to hunt wild fowl; the early hunters collaborated with packs of dogs to attack wild game too large for either to handle on their own.

Barloy gives a thought-provoking analysis of man's relationship with animals in our own time. Recent attempts to train dolphins for warfare are perhaps a new abuse of this relationship, while the breeding of a cross between the eland and the cow has produced a good milk-producer, immune to diseases spread by the tsetse fly. Man's need to understand and to be understood by animals retains an important hold on our daily lives.

ABOUT THE AUTHOR

Jean-Jacques Barloy is the natural history correspondent of *Le Monde* in Paris. Trained in natural science, he has devoted himself to a series of illuminating writings in this field, including an excellent study of *The world of birds*

MAN AND ANIMALS
100 Centuries of Friendship

J. J. Barloy

Translated by Henry Fox

GORDON & CREMONESI

© Editions France-Empire, 1974
First published in French as
LES ANIMAUX DOMESTIQUES
© Translation, Gordon Cremonesi Ltd 1978

Designed by Heather Gordon

Set in 12 on 13 pt Bembo
by Tradespools Ltd, Frome
and printed in Great Britain
by The Garden City Press Limited
Letchworth, Hertfordshire SG6 1JS

British Library Cataloguing in Publication Data
Barloy, J J
   Man and animals.
   1. Domestic animals—History   2. Animals and
   civilisation.
   I. Title   II. Fox, Henry
   636   SF41   77–30501
LCCN 77–030501
ISBN 0–86033-012-5

Gordon & Cremonesi Publishers
London and New York
New River House
34 Seymour Road
London N8 0BE

*The publishers wish to thank the Trustees of the British Museum and the School of
Oriental and African Studies, University of London, for their assistance and permission
to use illustrations included in this work.*

Table of Contents

For Muriel, Azu and co.
And Lillian, Bridie and Koshka.

In Place of a Foreword

FOR DAYS the snow has been falling on the immense plateau, which is now covered by a thick layer hiding rocks and gullies. All sounds are deadened by the steady fall of heavy flakes. Life itself seems to have ceased, and the very outlines of the landscape have receded into the distance. Yet, even in this cotton-wool atmosphere, a trained ear would have picked out the wing-beat of a flock of wild geese wheeling southward.

Half covered by the snow and hardened by frost, the carcass of a musk ox, ripped open by a bear, lies on the rocky ground. A lone mammoth makes his way through the blizzard in search of his herd, which he has lost in the storm. From time to time he can be heard calling desperately in the far distance, his voice sounding weaker and weaker . . .

Bent over double, dark red in the face, fingers numbed by the cold, Kaouhr and his friends, dressed in bear skins, carefully pick their way home to their tribe. They have to work hard to drag their feet out of the thick snow, and no sooner have they succeeded than they sink in again. They have little enough booty to bring back: only a few ptarmigan and grouse, which they have managed to approach thanks to the enveloping fog. The men trudge on. From time to time they shake off the snow which keeps gathering on their furs. It is not far now to the tribe—in normal weather it would take them a quarter of an hour. Soon the hunters reach the foot of a high, steep crag and then make their way round its base.

Suddenly Kaouhr signals his comrades to stop. Through the blizzard they can make out a slim shape about one hundred paces away, then a second and a third, and finally two more. The men know that what they can see are wild horses. The unexpected prize is tempting and they decide to try their luck. With infinite care, taking cover behind rocks and boulders, they manage to creep to within some 60 yards of the animals.

Kaouhr flexes his bow, the arrow whistles through the air, just missing the head of one of the horses . . . Alarmed by the attack, the beasts take flight. At that moment, rising on all sides, wild dogs appear. Haggard and starving, they converge on a mare and surround her. She tries to get away, but to no avail: the pack of dogs, their fangs bared, keep her at bay, terrifying her with their barking.

From there on, the mare is at the mercy of the hunters, who can now kill her with ease. The dogs at first slink away fearfully but hurry back once the coast is clear and devour the remains of the carcass left behind for them by the hunters as a reward.

In this way, step by step, a relationship based on mutual aid is built up between dog and man. Dog helps man to corner his quarry and keep it at bay and sometimes even drives the prey towards the hunters.

*   *   *

Centuries have passed. Not far from the place where Kaouhr and his friends were hunting, a village of houses on stilts has been built in the still waters of a lake. One day a little girl brings home a puppy whose parents have been killed. Her people are at first doubtful about taking in the stranger, but finally agree. The small animal proves easy to tame, and it is not long before it follows its new masters wherever they go.

*   *   *

There can be little doubt that one of the earliest processes of domestication known—that of the dog—passed through the two stages of evolution we have described in this story. Such, at any rate, is the view of the great Austrian biologist Konrad Lorenz.

But the dog is not the only animal to have become man's friend, for man has also succeeded in mastering many other species, from the cat to the oyster, from the horse to the bee, from the pig to the silkworm, not to speak of countless other mammals, birds and fishes.

It is the history of these processes of domestication we shall try to describe in this book. In their sum total, they amount to one of mankind's greatest adventures, an adventure which goes on to this day. Its impact on the course of history has been considerable: for instance, would there have been any knights if there had been no horses? And in our own time, the domestic pet must be seen as a major social phenomenon.

These varied and changing aspects of the domestication of animals add up to a fascinating story full of amazing episodes, both funny and tragic, solemn and ludicrous. But let us start by going back to the animal with which we began this foreword—man's best friend, the dog.

CHAPTER ONE

The Dog

MAN'S BEST friend is something of a
mystery to zoologists. As we have seen, the beginnings of his domestication are lost in the mists of time. What exactly were these animals
like which gradually came to be close associates of our ancestors?
Were they wolves, jackals or other wild members of the dog family?

It is hard to answer this question with any degree of exactitude.
This family of the *Canidae*, which even in our own day still includes
such wild animals as the Cape hunting dog, the coyote, the fox and
the fennec or desert fox, appears to be descended from a carnivorous
animal of the Oligocene—the *Cynodictis*. The genus *Canis*, which
includes both the dog and the wolf, made its appearance later, in the
Pliocene.

During the Pleistocene or Quaternary age—i.e. the era when man
first began to impose his mastery on the world—packs of *Canidae*
made contact with him in the way we have just described.

Undoubtedly, we are dealing here with a mere hypothesis, but one formulated by the great Austrian biologist Konrad Lorenz, who received the Nobel Prize in 1973 and became famous for his work on animal psychology. Observations made in Africa would seem to confirm his view: the pygmies, or negrillos, hunt with the aid of a half-wild dog, the Basenji, which drives game towards the hunter but itself remains free. For their services, the hunters throw the Basenji hunks of meat.

Just as the so-called 'primitive' peoples of our own day love to catch young animals without any apparent reason, it is quite possible that prehistoric man rounded up dogs and bred them. The Australian aborigines, in particular, capture dingo puppies—the yellow-brown dingo is the wild dog of Australia—and keep them for a time before letting them loose.

According to Lorenz, the dog has two character traits which make him easy to train. Above all, he is sociable and instinctively tends to attach himself to the leader of the pack. Step by step, he has come to look upon man as his leader. Dogs are said to retain throughout their lives another childhood characteristic: to them, their master is their mother.

Archaeological and palaeontological discoveries, too, have provided evidence of the origin of the house dog. Recent successes in determining the age of archaeological finds by means of the carbon-14[1] technique have tended to confirm Lorenz's views. By means of this method it was discovered that a number of dog skeletons—found at Argissa in Greece and Sarab in Iran and known, as a result of supporting evidence, to be those of domesticated animals—date from 7000 B.C. There can also be no doubt that it did not take long before distinct breeds began to emerge. Remains of two types of dog which date from the same period as those mentioned above have, in fact, been found in northern Europe, notably at the Maglemose site in Denmark.

The first dog, known as Small Maglemose or Peat dog, fairly closely resembled the jackal, his probable ancestor. He must have looked somewhat like the present-day Samoyed, i.e. he had a short muzzle, a broad chest and long legs.

The Great Maglemose, on the other hand, was a big animal, undoubtedly descended from the wolf, and had powerful jaws and a pointed muzzle. Remains of these dogs have been discovered at the sites of lake settlements in the Alps.

The question is: were these two breeds already domesticated? One fact indicates that they were. Marks found on certain bone specimens unearthed at prehistoric sites in Denmark could only have been made by the teeth of dogs. These bones have clearly been gnawed by dogs over and over again. Therefore, the dogs could not possibly have been wild. And in Russia, a neolithic[2] skeleton of a dog has been found resembling that of a dingo.

The Lepenski Vir site in the Danube Valley on the Yugoslav–Rumanian border, which is known to be 6,000 years old, has attracted a great deal of attention among researchers in recent years. It contains bones of various animals we know to have been domesticated at that time—bulls, pigs, sheep, etc. and, above all, dogs. Those found in the oldest strata all belong to small dogs, while those present in the most recent layer come from larger breeds. However, fewer bones of large dogs have been found than of small ones.

Archaeologists have asked themselves for what purpose the Lepenski Vir dogs were bred. They were not used to guard herds, since there were none at that time (at least not at the beginning of the period from which the site dates), nor were they used to guard houses, for these were built very close to one another and there was thus no need to keep guard dogs. It follows that these dogs must have been used for hunting, and no doubt they were also eaten by the people of the region.

While man was gaining mastery over the dog in various parts of Eurasia, an identical process was taking place on the opposite side of the Mediterranean, as we know from the rock paintings found in the Tassili mountains in the Sahara. These, too, depict two distinct breeds: a greyhound—the ancestor of the greyhounds found today in Spain and Provence; and a comparatively large dog with shortish legs, a big head and short nose.

*   *   *

At the dawn of history, the domestication of the dog was thus already well advanced. The Sumerians and Assyrians of Mesopotamia had dogs of a type which later spread right across the world. The bas-reliefs of Assurbanipal show these terrifying beasts, used for hunting wild pig and horses. The famous Saint Bernard also originates from Mesopotamia.

The dog is barely mentioned in the Bible, which, in the main depicts him as an unclean beast. However, it was dogs who drove away the vultures devouring Abel's body, and dogs guarded the flocks of sheep mentioned in the Book of Job. Both Arabs and Jews owned dogs from the bronze age onwards.

The dog played a much more important role in ancient Egypt. As early as 4240 B.C., the God Set was venerated as a greyhound with a forked tail, while the God Anubis was depicted as a man with a dog's or a jackal's head. The God Khentamentiou of Abydos, later identified with Osiris, was depicted as a dog.

At about 2600 B.C. dogs began to be included in hunting scenes. The *stele* of Antifaa II, a Pharaoh of the Tenth Dynasty, shows him accompanied by dogs of four distinct breeds: a greyhound, a mastiff, a dog resembling the Australian Dingo, and a small dog. The Egyptian greyhound, which had straight ears, an unusually narrow chest and inward curling tail, is the ancestor of two splendid breeds which have survived to this day, the Arabian gazelle hound and the Saluki or Persian greyhound. The first of these was called 'the king of dogs and the dog of kings'. It had a long head, straight legs and a smooth coat, usually sandy-coloured, and was found throughout North Africa and the Sahara.

The Saluki is probably the breed which has inspired more artists than any other. Effigies of this smooth-haired greyhound, with its fringed ears and tail, have been found in many parts of Egypt and Mesopotamia. The Pharaoh Antef owned a Saluki, whom he called 'White Gazelle'. King Solomon and Cleopatra were both fond of the breed, which subsequently became popular among the Arabs and Persians. Mohammed owned a white Saluki. The Arabs, who despised dogs, made an exception of this breed, which they named *al-baraka*, or 'the blessed one'. The Arabs of Africa to this day treat the Gazelle hound as a noble animal. The Bedouin use the Saluki for hunting, as it can reach the incredible speed of 80 km an hour, and is able to catch gazelles. Nomads occasionally use both falcons and the Saluki together. The English crusaders introduced the breed into Europe. Again it inspired artists: Veronese included a Saluki in a painting which may be seen in Turin.

But let us return to ancient Egypt. The first Basset hounds appeared during the Middle Kingdom. They owed their existence to one of the earliest mutations known to history. At that time, the Egyptians used to play the 'dog game', a precursor of our present-day backgammon. In a later age, the Hyksos seem to have imported their formidable mastiffs into Egypt. They were used by the Egyptians in battle. These dogs, with spiked collars round their necks, would be sent to attack the Egyptians' enemies.

The Egyptians adored their dogs. They gave them gilt leather collars, adorned with designs and hieroglyphic inscriptions, and when the animals died, they would sometimes be mummified and placed in sarcophagi. Dog mummies have even been found wearing death masks and collars made of flowers.

In Phoenicia, the God Baal was often depicted with a dog's head. As long ago as the neolithic age, the Hittites used dogs for hunting, particularly stag and lion. A curious habit has survived until our times at Catal Hüyük, in Turkey, where the people ward off bad luck by placing the skull of a sheep dog, together with a few grains of ripe seed, in a prominent place in the backyard. In Persia, it used to be forbidden to kill dogs, who were known as 'sons of the fire'. The word for dog, *Chan*, was bestowed on persons of great importance. In India, the mastiff was known at about 280 B.C. The 'Roof of the World' was the home of the biggest dog there has ever been, the Tibetan mastiff, which stood as tall as a small donkey. Marco Polo tells us he saw one of these animals. Descendants of this breed have survived into our own age; they have large heads, small, drooping ears and a black coat. They are, however, smaller than their ancestor, which has now disappeared.

*   *   *

In Greece, the dog was at first not regarded very highly, as we can see from the term κυνισμός (*kynismos*). This word, itself derived from κύων (*kyon*), i.e. dog, originally meant 'contempt for good manners'. The word has since acquired the connotation we associate with 'cynicism'. Later, however, the animal won great respect and, to attract attention among the Athenians, Alcibiades could think of no more striking—if not particularly clever—'publicity stunt' than to cut off the tail of his fine dog.

Homer sings the praises of Ulysses' old dog, which patiently waited for its master's return and died as soon as he got back. Dogs play a considerable part in Greek mythology: thus the God of Fire,

Vulcan, forged a brass dog which he brought to life and presented to Zeus. The latter gave it to Europa, the daughter of the Phoenician King Agenor. Another famous dog of Greek mythology was the terrible Cerberus, of which more later. The dog was sacred to Hecate, a goddess of Thracian origin.

A dog was trained by Apollo and was the hunting companion of Artemis. A statue of the goddess's greyhound, with its slim figure, recalls the big greyhound of Upper Egypt.

In Rome, dogs were used for a great variety of tasks. They were, for instance, employed as scavengers to clean the streets, which were smothered in dirt, due to the inadequacy of the municipal sewerage system. It was in Rome that dogs began their career as guard animals. The warning notice *Cave canem* (Beware of the Dog) advised visitors that a 'vicious dog' was guarding the house. Public buildings in Rome were guarded by mastiffs.

However the Romans also kept dogs as pets. Housewives would take their small dogs for walks on leads through the streets of the city. The small Italian greyhound appears to have been particularly popular. A painting found in Herculaneun would seem to indicate that guide dogs for the blind were already in use in those days. In the city of Adranon, in Sicily, a thousand large, sacred dogs were kept in the precincts of a temple sacred to the God Adranos: their task was to guide drunkards home at night.

The Romans also used dogs to carry messages. These were placed inside metal tubes which the animals were forced to swallow. Alas, the recovery of these messages cost them their lives. Some experts believe that the Romans may already have had dog cemeteries. In 1929 dog skeletons dating from the reign of the Emperor Domitian were discovered, and coins were found among these remains.

The ancient Gauls are known to have owned dogs, whom they used in their curious rite of the flaming wheel. The latter was made to roll down a hillside, through a stream—where the fire was quenched—and up the opposite slope. Dogs were tied to this wheel, which symbolised the revolving 'fire of heaven'. The Gauls also used dogs in battle and, above all, for hunting. They were used to hunt hare and stag, and the interest lay more in the pursuit of the quarry than its capture.

*   *   *

The Middle Ages began badly for the dog. After the fall of the Roman Empire, people again regarded them with contempt. Packs of wild dogs roamed the countryside, stripping corpses of flesh. This was the time of legends such as that of the 'hound of hell'; it was in those days, too, that the French term of invective *canaille*, which comes from the Latin word for dog (*canis*), was coined.

Before very long, however, the animal regained its popularity—thanks to hunting. Monasteries devoted themselves to the breeding of hunting dogs, and it was in the Abbey of St. Hubert, in the Ardennes, that the breed of that name was established. The St. Hubert stands 75 cm high and has a dark coat and drooping ears. It was at that time also that people began to look after their dogs properly.

The landed gentry lavished affection on their dogs and even took them to church for mass. When this practice was forbidden under Charlemagne, they took to attending the services from outside the church, the doors of which would be left open for their benefit. An Order of the Dog was created by Baron Lissoire de Montmorency.

In some countries, this attachment to dogs led to strange abberrations. Thus, in the eleventh century a dog sat on the throne of Norway. The facts are not in dispute: the King, to revenge himself on his subjects, who had deposed him, left them with the choice of having either a slave or a dog as their next King. They chose a dog, which was given the name of Saur I and was from then on treated in every way as King, with a court, bodyguard and officers. When it rained the courtiers would take his canine majesty into their arms to make sure his paws did not get wet. He even signed decrees! Alas, a wolf's fangs put an end to this splendid reign. Hungary, we are told, went through much the same experience.

Then came the Crusades, and the Crusaders took their hounds with them to the Orient. There, the animals were crossed with greyhounds, and it was thus that the first spaniels came into being. St. Louis imported the Oriental greyhound into Europe. The breeds of hunting dogs continued to increase in number and diversity. The French spaniel was taught to flatten his body against the ground so as to avoid the nets thrown by the hunters, thus becoming the first setter.

*   *   *

Books on dogs first appeared during the Renaissance, when dogs enjoyed great esteem. They were allowed to take part in the *Kermesse* festivals in Flanders, and were also popular in Italy. 'In Venice', we are told by Dr. Fernand Méry in his book *Le Chien, son mystère* (Pont-Royal, 1970), 'ornate gondolas glide silently over the greenish-blue canals. Every now and then we see one carrying a lady—on her way to some palace, no doubt—gazing tenderly at her light-haired toy dog (known as Florentine), sitting in the bows for all the world like a ship's figurehead.' These lap dogs were usually of either the Maltese or the Teneriffe breeds. The Maltese, by the way, dates from classical antiquity.

The dog, at the same time, continued to play a military role. Henry VIII used more than 500 hounds in a battle against Charles V. At that time, too, a dog of less impressive size, the curly Maltese, first made its appearance in England. Other breeds were used as turnspits.

The greyhound, that splendid breed, was used in a field sport which became very popular in those days—coursing. Two dogs were set to chase a hare, and the winning animal was the one which forced the hare to make the most turns.

In France, to own a 'King's White Dog' was the height of fashion. Gaston Phébus, Comte de Foix, called these huge beasts *les bauds*—the 'bold ones'. The breed was probably a cross between the white St. Hubert and the Italian Brach hound. Packs of these dogs were owned by Francis I of France and his successors.

Henry III of France, on the other hand, was fond of the *Papillon*, a dwarf spaniel. The King would often go for walks carrying one of these animals in a basket hanging from his neck. These toy dogs had erect ears, unlike the dwarf spaniel favoured by King Charles I of England, which had drooping ears.

In the eighteenth century the Brach hounds were all the rage, and at the same time more and more packs of hounds were established. It was about then that the Barbet, a dog used for hunting over marshy ground, underwent a change as a result of a chance mutation. The new breed, which had a curly coat, became popular as our poodle.

Towards the end of the eighteenth century, the Basset hound became fashionable again, and at the same time the Breton spaniel made its appearance. In England the first Setters—and later the Pointers—were seen, the latter probably a cross between the greyhound and the Brach.

In 1807, a new breed, the Chesapeake Bay, came into being in strange circumstances. In that year a British ship was wrecked on the coast of Maryland. Some passengers gave two Newfoundland puppies they had on board to local people, who crossed them with retrievers of a type found in the area, and the Chesapeake Bay breed was born.

The Pug was greatly prized in France in the reign of King Louis-Philippe. This small dog, with a short muzzle and bulging eyes, was given its French name of *Carlin* because it reminded people of an Italian actor of that name.

The Pekinese, which became popular at the Chinese Imperial Court, was introduced into Europe in 1860. Twenty years later the Scottish Skye terrier became fashionable. At first its legs were of normal length, but subsequently a short-legged variety was bred. The Corgi, the breed which enjoys royal patronage in England, became popular at the same time. With its 'foxy' look, it is both endearing and amusing. Later it was the turn of the Bulldog to make its appearance.

The twentieth century saw the beginning of *cynology*—the science of the dog—and a vast increase in the number of dog shows. After the 1914–18 war, several breeds popular in Germany were introduced into France, such as the Boxer, the Doberman Pinscher and the Alsatian, and after the 1939–45 war the Dachshund won great acclaim among French dog lovers. In the late 'fifties, the Dalmatian —a dog whose coat looks as if it had been spotted with ink— experienced a short-lived vogue.

*   *   *

One breed deserves special mention: the St. Bernard. First, because it is the biggest dog bred at present and, secondly, because of its remarkable history. This huge animal has a massive but short head and drooping ears, a white-and-red brindled coat, with two typical red marks around the eyes. It measures up to 80 cm at the shoulder and can weigh up to 100 kg.

As has been mentioned, the breed originates from ancient Mesopotamia, and examples of it can be seen portrayed on Assyrian *bas-reliefs*. From Mesopotamia, it spread first to Greece and then to Rome, where it was used as a guard dog. The St. Bernard was imported into the Alps by the Romans during the Gallic wars and, isolated in the high valleys, the breed has continued there more or less unchanged to this day.

It was in 1660 that it was first introduced into the Hospice of St. Bernard, now situated in Swiss territory. St. Bernard himself, who lived in the tenth century, thus never saw one of these dogs, and it is an anachronism to portray the saint in the company of these animals. In the Hospice, the St. Bernards were at first used as guard dogs and subsequently in the kitchen, where they were put to work as 'turnspits', treading a wheel. Towards 1750, the monks first began training the dogs for their task of saving the lives of travellers lost in the mountains. The monk who supervises this work is known as *marronier*, and his job is to teach the dog to make a trail in the snow with his broad chest.

The most famous St. Bernard of all times was Barry. Born at the beginning of the nineteenth century, he saved more than forty lives in twelve years. In a book about the breed, Canon Marquis writes of Barry: 'Legend has it that one day he came across a little boy lost in the snow. We are told that he licked the child's face and persuaded him, we do not know how, to climb on his back. At all events, the child got on the dog's back and was safely carried by Barry to the Hospice. Who is to say—perhaps the legend is true!' Barry ended his days in 1814 in Berne—contrary to a tenacious myth according to which he was killed by a traveller who mistook him for a bear. Barry's mortal remains are in fact on show in Berne in the Natural History Museum.

There is a continuing tradition in the Hospice kennels of naming the finest male dog after Barry. Despite this, *Turc* and *Lion* became famous in the last century, and paintings of them can be seen in the Hospice. About the year 1800 the Canons of the Great St. Bernard Hospice offered some of the animals to European dog-lovers. In Switzerland it is held that a pure St. Bernard must have a smooth coat, but in Britain the rough-haired variety is more popular. One thing is certain, it is to a Swiss breeder, H. Schumacher, that we owe the survival of the pure breed.

Since the beginning of this century, the Hospice has been keeping between twelve and thirty dogs. Two of the animals have acquired enduring fame: Barry II, who was invariably at the head of his rescue team and was lost in a crevasse in 1905, and Barry III, who fell into a ravine five years later.

Since those days, the Hospice has tightened up its selection procedure and improved its care of the animals. The dogs themselves are kept in well-aired kennels and exercised each morning and evening in large grounds kept up specially for their benefit. The St. Bernard puppies are immensely popular with tourists. In the winter, only the dogs used for rescue operations remain in the Hospice; the others are taken down into the plain. To conclude this section, perhaps we should mention a breed closely related to the St. Bernard—the Pyrenean mountain dog.

From what we have said it follows that during the course of history dogs have been used for a wide range of tasks. In Northern France and Belgium dogs were at one time employed pulling carts, and in the Arctic regions of Asia and America they are to this day used to pull sleighs.

The strong Husky—a dog with a thick coat and coiled tail—can cover distances of 50–60 km a day in the icy wastes of Greenland. The teams are harnessed fan-wise, with anything up to ten or twelve huskies tied singly to a sleigh. In Siberia, on the other hand, the entire team is harnessed to a single line, with the dogs arranged alternately one on the left and one on the right. From the Arctic, the husky was introduced into the Antarctic, where it has given good service to explorers.

The best known husky used by French explorers in Adelie Land in the Antarctic was Boss. He was lead dog for no less than ten years—a rare distinction—for in general no dog retains this position for more than four to five years. In the end he had to give way to one of his own progeny, Fram the Bold. Boss was 'repatriated' to France, and ended his life in a villa near Paris, where he died—after catching a cold!

*   *   *

Dogs now perform a whole new range of tasks. The Labrador, for instance—a splendid black or golden smooth-haired dog—is employed at airports to detect drugs. In the U.S.S.R., Alsatians, thanks to their outstanding sense of smell, are used to discover mineral deposits: they can spot them to a depth of 12 m.

The Husky, like its masters, originates from Asia. So far, in our history of the dog, we have not spoken of America. It was about 8400 B.C. that dogs made their way to that continent in the wake of hordes of yellow-skinned invaders—the future 'Indians'—who got there from Siberia by way of Alaska.

In 1966, in Missouri, the skeleton of a small adult dog was uncovered buried under a stone cairn, showing that the dog had at one time been the object of religious ritual. At the time of the Incas, four breeds of domesticated dogs were kept in America.[3] Dogs play a part in Indian art and legend, and were sacrificed and mummified. The Sioux used them for hunting, while in the Andes they were employed to guard herds of llamas. A bald breed, the Ch'ono, is known to have existed before Columbus discovered America. Two specimens, a male and a female, have recently been discovered living in Peru. The only hair to be found on the entire body of this strange beast is in two tufts—one at the top of the head and the other at the point of the tail. The two Ch'onos have produced three puppies which are being closely studied by experts.

Let us now turn to the Chihuahua. This tiny dog—which never stands more than 20 cm tall or exceeds 2 kg in weight—enjoys great popularity. It is believed to originate from Mexico, but there can be no doubt that it was unknown both to the Mayas and the Aztecs. Apart from its baldness, the animal closely resembles the Papillon. The following theory has been put forward to explain its background:

After the conquest of Mexico by Spain, a trade route was established linking Peking with Madrid by way of America. Quite possibly, therefore, miniature dogs from China and the European Papillon were introduced into Mexico at one and the same time. The mysterious Chihuahua—which may well be the most fashionable toy dog of the future—could therefore be a cross between these two breeds.

*   *   *

In 1973 a new breed received official recognition in France and is known there as *Eurasier*. This was an event of some importance to French dog-lovers, for it was the first time in thirty years that a new breed had been officially registered in their country. The breed, which originates from Germany, is called *Eurasier* since it is a cross between a European and an Asian breed, the Chow-chow and the Wolf-Spitz—the latter being a robust breed from Northern Europe. The *Eurasier* is a large dog; its body, with its shaggy coat, resembles that of a bear cub, while its head recalls that of a wolf. Its coat is usually reddish brown, and occasionally black. The selection was carried out not only with an eye to appearance but also—and mainly—to the animal's character, and this in fact is its most interesting feature. In the course of selection, animals of a nervous disposition were eliminated from successive generations. The result was a breed noted for its calm and even temper and it is thus an ideal playmate for children. The *Eurasier* neither bites nor barks and is the very soul of obedience.

*   *   *

It goes without saying that dogs feature in many myths and legends. In French folklore, the dog usually plays the part of a phantom which barks in the night. At Antrenas in the Lozère Department, a black dog, said to harbour the soul of one of the lords of the manor seeking admittance to his ancestral domain, pads round and round the local castle at night. In Bayeux, in the Calvados, a dog roams through the night, dragging chains behind it. Touch it with a key and lo and behold, it resumes human shape, for it is a sorcerer who has been changed into a dog! These legends are closely associated with lycanthropy, the belief that wolves sometimes assume human shape. At Wissembourg, in Alsace, a black dog with a key in its mouth stands guard over a treasure.

One of the best known of French legends is the one about the Dog of Montargis. This folk tale, which is devoid of any historical foundation whatever, is derived from a *chanson de geste*—or ballad—called *The Song of Macaire,* which owes some of its fame to Montaigne.

Blanchefleur, the mythical wife of Charlemagne and daughter of the Emperor of Byzantium, was courted by the knight Macaire. She rejected his advances, whereupon Macaire decided to take his revenge. He bribed the Queen's dwarf, inducing him to pretend he had been Blanchefleur's lover. Charlemagne, convinced that he had been cuckolded, condemned his wife to be burnt at the stake. On second thoughts, for fear of reprisals from his father-in-law, he thought better of it and decided to send Blanchefleur home. She was duly dispatched to Byzantium, with the knight Aubry, who took his greyhound Verbaux along on the journey, as her escort. On their way through a forest, the travellers were attacked by Macaire, who wished to abduct the Queen. Aubry did his best to defend her, but was mortally wounded. Macaire buried him under a tree and then started looking for the Queen, who had in the meantime taken flight, and he failed to find her. The faithful Verbaux stayed behind for three days, guarding his master's grave, before returning to Paris. Once back in the capital, the faithful dog made straight for the Palace, where Charlemagne and his retinue happened to be dining, with Macaire among the guests. The dog leapt at his throat and tried to kill him on the spot, but Macaire was saved in the nick of time by some of the other guests.

Verbaux then led Charlemagne and his suite to the scene of the crime, where they found Aubry's body. Since Macaire denied his guilt, the Emperor decided that the suspect and the dog should confront one another in a duel.

Macaire was armed with a cudgel, while the dog was given an empty cask for cover. Verbaux won the contest. He pinned his adversary to the ground and gripped him by the throat with his teeth. The murderer thereupon admitted his guilt and was executed the following day. All Charlemagne now had to do was to retrieve his Blanchefleur, who had in the meantime reached Byzantium. An engraving which pictures the duel between Macaire and Verbaux has since become famous and can be seen in the Museum at Montargis, and as a result the legend has become popularly known as 'The Dog of Montargis'.

*   *   *

Countless legends feature dogs as guardians of the Gates of Hell. A visit to what we might call the kennels 'down below' is particularly instructive, for it shows that this theme occurs among nations the world over.

The most renowned of these Hounds of Hell is without doubt Cerberus—usually depicted as a three-headed beast, though he has been credited with no fewer than fifty heads. Cerberus is either to be found by the banks of a black river or guarding the entrance to the palace of his master, Pluto, God of the Dead. With his three mouths, he jealously guards the Gates of Hell, not allowing the living to pass but only the dead, and even they can enter only after they have given Cerberus the honey cakes which the mourners who attended their funerals had placed in their graves. Appeased by this offering, Cerberus allows them to pass. Those, however, who attempt to escape from Hell, he devours.

The legend of Cerberus has inspired many poets. In his *Divine Comedy*, Dante describes the monster he saw on his voyage through Hell:

> Cerberus, the cruel, misshapen monster,
>   there
> Bays in his triple gullet and doglike
>   growls
> Over the wallowing shades; his eyeballs
>   glare
>
> A bloodshot crimson, and his bearded
>   jowls
> Are greasy and black; pot-bellied, talon-
>   heeled,
> He clutches and flays and rips and rends
>   the souls.[4]

In his *Poèmes barbares*, Leconte de Lisle describes the Guardian of Hell:

> Horrible, beautiful monster of Krysaor's
>   womb,
> She, mother of Kerberos of the fifty jaws,
> Kerberos, ever hungering by dark, ebony
>   waves
> Howling at the dead who know no tomb.

Cerberus sprang from the union of Typhon, the God of Disaster, and Echidna, a monster half-woman and half-serpent. It was this same union which brought forth the Chimaera, the Gorgon, the Scylla, the Hydra of Lerna, the Nemean Lion and more creatures of the same ilk. This remarkable family could boast among its members one other dog, the twin-headed Orthus, who guarded King Geryon's herd of red oxen and was slain by Hercules.

Several heroes managed to get the better of the terrible Cerberus. Orpheus charmed him by playing his lyre to him and thus succeeded in entering Hell, to look for his young wife Eurydice. The Gods had made an exception of him and gave him permission to enter Hell, but on condition that he would not look at Eurydice before returning to Earth. Alas, Orpheus glanced backwards too soon and Eurydice vanished for ever into the darkness.

Bacchus (Dionysos) was more fortunate; he succeeded in snatching his mother from the jaws of Hell at the cost of a single live sheep which he gave to the three-headed monster as his entrance fee. Hercules, as the twelfth of his labours, was ordered to capture Cerberus alive. He was given permission by Pluto to make the attempt, on condition that he did not use any weapons. The hero got hold of the dog by his neck, and, disregarding the bites of the dragon which Cerberus had in place of a tail, he brought the Hound of Hell with him back to Earth. Hercules showed Cerberus to Eurystheus, King of Mycenae, who had ordered him to undertake the feat, and then took him back to Hell.

Similar legends are current among the American Indians. Thus, the story used to be told that before they can enter the hereafter, the dead must first cross a stream, clinging to a slippery tree trunk. Those among them who during their lifetimes had been unkind, especially to dogs, were dragged off the trunk and thrown into the water by a mastiff.

The Aztecs, who used to breed dogs with golden coats the colour of the sun, would kill the animals on the death of their master so that they might help him cross the nine rivers which guard the Gates of Hell. This was in fact a variant of the earlier legend of the dog-god Xolotl, who accompanied the Sun on his journey to the Land of the Dead.

In India, according to Parsee legend, the dead must cross the Bridge of Cinvat (or Bridge of Judgment), which spans the River of Destiny. Demons and gods fight over the souls of the travellers. The gods are helped by dogs to make sure that only the souls of the good enter Paradise while those of the evil fall into a bottomless pit. Again, those who have killed dogs during their lifetimes must expect no mercy.

It is in India too, that the great God Indra uses the bitch Sâramâ as his messenger. Sâramâ's two redoubtable sons, the Sârameyâu, are the messengers of Yama, God of Death. Their task is to guide the souls of the dead to their last resting place. It used to be customary, therefore,

for the bereaved to place rice cakes or cow's kidneys in the hands of
the dead, in the hope that these offerings would please the dogs.

The *Rigveda*, the sacred Book of India, describes the two beasts as
follows: 'They have four eyes and a speckled skin . . . these most
savage guardians who watch the path and observe the people; they,
of the huge nostrils, deep lungs and great strength, they, the
messengers of Yama.' The more cruel of the two is 'resplendent, with
reddish teeth which, well rooted in their gums, sound like the clash of
lances when they meet'.

In his poem *Prière védique pour les Morts*, Leconte de Lisle renders this
picture in these words:

> Close, oh shepherd of the world, the
>   deathly lids
>
> Of Yama's twin hounds who haunt the
>   shades
> . . . Let the divine Shepherd put his
>   mighty dogs to flight
>
> Who howling prowl the path of men of
>   right
> . . . Blind, oh shepherd of the world,
>   with your burning hands
>
> The bloody eyes of Yama's hounds.
>
> Oh, that your dogs, to whom sleep
>   was never known,
> And whose broad nostrils track down
>   every race,
> Might, till the last awakening dawn,
> In the hills and valleys lose our trace
> And leave us long to contemplate the
>   splendour of the sun.

Sâramâ, the mother of the two dogs, is sometimes confused with
another female Hound of Hell, Sarvara or Carvara, whose name
strangely echoes that of Cerberus.

Anubis, the Egyptian God of the Tombs—who is depicted with the head of either a dog or a jackal—would guide the souls of the dead to their last resting place and help Osiris decide their fate. Every soul was placed in a balance before the assembled gods, and Anubis would announce the result: the souls whose good deeds outweighed their misdeeds had a right to eternal bliss. Anubis was, in addition, the presiding spirit of the art of embalming. He was venerated at Samallut, which the Greeks later called Cynopolis, the City of the Dogs.

The Germanic peoples, too, had their Hound of Hell—the terrible Garm (the greedy one)—a monstrous beast which guarded the Gates of Hell. Garm, whose chest was bespattered with blood, was the dog of Hel, the Goddess of Death. He was merciless in his treatment of those of the dead who had been unkind while they dwelt upon earth. The souls of the kind, on the other hand, were not only permitted to pass but even allowed to keep whatever presents they might have brought with them. This dog, like the other Germanic godheads, was destined to perish in the famous Twilight of the Gods, the *Goetterdaemmerung*.

As we have seen, mythical dogs abound in the folklore of several regions of Europe. One such legend was used by Arthur Conan Doyle in his masterpiece *The Hound of the Baskervilles*. In his story, Conan Doyle tells of a monstrous dog which roamed the moors and fell upon the last surviving descendant of a noble family. The mystery was solved by the legendary Sherlock Holmes.

[1] The technique is briefly as follows: it takes 5,600 years for one half of the carbon-14 or radioactive carbon present in any one organism to disappear; 11,200 years for three-quarters; 16,800 years for seven-eighths, etc. The amount of carbon-14 present in a fossil thus enables us to determine its age.

[2] The neolithic was the final stage of the prehistoric age; it was followed first by the bronze and then the iron age. Together these constitute the proto-historic period.

[3] The Amerindians began to domesticate the dog at a relatively early stage and crossed their animals with various other members of the dog family such as the Maned wolf and the Crab-eating hyena to produce new breeds for hunting.

[4] Translation by Dorothy L. Sayers, Penguin Books, 1971.

CHAPTER TWO

The Cat

COMPARED WITH the dog, whose domestication is lost in the mists of time, the cat is something of a newcomer. It was only at the dawn of history that man succeeded in taming it. We shall encounter the people in question—the ancient Egyptians—at all stages of our history of the domestication of animals, for they were past masters of this art.

We can, thus, give a fairly precise idea of the time and place of the cat's domestication, but its ancestry presents a much more difficult problem. It is certainly not descended from the European wild cat, which undoubtedly exists in much larger numbers than people tend to realise. The cat's ancestor is far more likely to have been the 'gloved' Libyan cat (*Felis libyca*), an animal with a spotted coat whose habitat—as the name implies—is North Africa. It must be said, however, that not all the experts agree with this hypothesis. Some believe that the cat is descended from the panther, and the cat's supple movements undoubtedly remind us of that beast. Other scientists have suggested that the cat might be descended from a 'mini-panther'.

The cat of ancient Egypt resembled more than any other animal the cheetah of our own day. Thanks to the many paintings and sculptures which have survived,[1] we know fairly precisely what it looked like. It had a slim, elongated body, with a narrow chest, long legs, straight shoulders and a serpentlike head. Its coat tended to be striped, though occasionally the stripes were confined to the paws and tail. These characteristics form a link between the Egyptian and the Abyssinian cat, which has displaced the former in Egypt and can be found there to this day roaming the marshes.

It was probably some time before 2500 B.C., i.e. during the Fifth Dynasty, that the cat was domesticated. At about that time, too, cats first made their appearance in temples, where they replaced the lionesses which had previously been used there as guard animals. A painting which dates from that time shows a cat sufficiently tame to wear a collar.

Before very long, people began to worship the cat. The lioness-goddess Sekmet made way for the cat goddess Bastet, one of the most important figures in the Egyptian pantheon. Her name means: 'She who rends the flesh', or 'She who brings back the booty'. She was also given the flattering epithets of 'Mother of Beauty', 'Lady of Heaven' and 'Goddess of Love', and was said to be a daughter of Isis and Osiris.

It was under the Twenty-second Dynasty that the cult of Bastet became most widespread. A temple—described by Herodotus—was dedicated to her at Bubastis. A statue of Bastet stood in the centre of the temple, where a festival was held each year. Bastet was usually depicted with a cat's head, though occasionally she was shown with the head of a lion. She had pointed—at times even bat-like—ears. Her emblems were a basket, a musical instrument (the sistrum) and a shield (the aegis). Another cat goddess was venerated by the Egyptians at Speos Artemidos, near Beni-Hasan.

There was a statue of Bastet in every Egyptian home. All young married couples owned amulets representing the goddess together with a number of kittens. This was tantamount to a prayer to Bastet to send them the equivalent number of children. The cat symbolised the fertility of the earth; paradoxically, however, it was at the same time a symbol of virginity. Bastet herself was believed to be a virgin.

This symbolism is thought to have been inspired by the animal's great cleanliness.

Many Egyptians believed themselves to be descended from a cat. Women would go out of their way to move slinkily like cats, rather like our present-day 'vamps'; Cleopatra herself indulged in this fad. An extraordinary ritual was observed when children were dedicated to the goddess Bastet. First, the silhouette of a cat was tattooed on the child's arm; a priest would then make an incision level with the tattoo mark, whereupon a few drops of a cat's blood were sprinkled on the wound. The blending of the two types of blood symbolised the union between child and goddess.

When a cat died accidentally in a public place, any bystanders would get down on their knees, loudly protesting that they were not responsible. When a cat died a natural death, its owners would shave off their eyebrows as a sign of mourning and give vent to their grief with much weeping and sighing.

They would hold a wake over the little corpse, close the cat's eyes and press its whiskers back against the lips, adorn it with a turquoise collar and bind it with thongs. The cat would then be embalmed and placed in a sarcophagus. In 1889, a fellah discovered a *necropolis*, or city of the dead, at Beni-Hasan, containing the mummies of some 300,000 cats. The remains were sent to England, where people could find no use for them other than to turn them into fertiliser.

The Egyptians used to mummify their cats because the animals were believed to possess miraculous powers over demons. A papyrus by the scribe Hunefer, dating from the Ninth Dynasty, shows a cat in the act of beheading Apopi, the Serpent of the Night. Apopi was an incarnation of Set, God of Darkness; the latter sought to capsize the boat ferrying the dead in order to seize his soul. Another papyrus shows a cat side by side with a scarab, symbol of light and creation.

The 'murder' of a cat was punishable by death. Kambyses, King of Persia, and son of Cyrus the Great, turned the awe in which cats were held by the Egyptians to his advantage. In 525 B.C., when his troops were laying siege to the Egyptian city of Pelusium and there seemed to be no chance of an early success, he ordered his men to catch all the cats in the district. When the Persian soldiers appeared, each clutching a cat against his chest, the Egyptian defenders were afraid to fire on the attackers protected by these live shields. The city fell to Kambyses without further resistance.

The loving care with which the Egyptians surrounded their cats did not prevent them from making use of the animals for practical ends. They used them for hunting—not rodents, as you might expect—but ducks. The owners would take their cats along with them in a boat. Held on a lead, the cats would comb the papyrus marshes for birds. And to this day, if you allow a cat anywhere near a papyrus plant, it will gnaw it and breathe in its aroma avidly, and once it has done so will always be on the look-out for more. Dr. Fernand Méry has put forward the theory that the cat may have retained among its genetical heritage a 'memory' of the distant past when its ancestors used to hunt through the papyrus thickets.

The cat played a role in many other rites and beliefs. Thus Bastet was at one and the same time Goddess of the Sun and of the Moon. This latter belief, which also occurs in other civilisations, is comparatively easy to explain: in the dark, the two eyes of the cat resemble two small moons. In the temples consecrated to the moon, the priests used to breed cats, and Bastet was eventually taken over by the Greeks and transformed into Artemis, Goddess of the Moon.

The Egyptians used to attribute healing powers to the cat: Bastet was believed to be able to cure those suffering from snake bite. Conversely, in the Metropolitan Museum in New York you can see a column covered with such inscriptions as 'Charm to dispel poison affecting cat'. This must have been a talisman used to heal a cat stung by a scorpion.

*   *   *

From Egypt, the cat spread right across the world, both east and west. In Asia, it reached the Middle East, although it is barely mentioned in the Bible, and where the Bible does speak of cats it is as symbols of treachery and deceit. In the Book of Baruch, Jeremiah warns the Jews captive in Babylon not to be deceived by heathen idols:

> Owls flutter above their bodies and heads, and swallows and other birds, too, and cats frolic upon them. Hence you can see that these are not gods. Therefore, fear them not.

Among the Arabs, the cat was more highly regarded. Before the coming of Islam, the Arabs used to worship a golden cat. Islam itself holds the cat in high esteem, no doubt in memory of Muezza, the Prophet's beloved cat. In the thirteenth century, the authorities in Cairo ordered that food should be distributed each day among the city's stray cats. In the Islamic countries, cats are even permitted to enter mosques.

In the India of about 400 B.C., all animals were protected by Buddhism except the cat, for the cat, when called upon—together with all other living beings—to be present when the Buddha entered Nirvana[2] had fallen asleep on the way and had therefore arrived late. Another legend explains why, in China and Japan, the cat was excluded from the group of animals featured in the Zodiac: when all the animals had gathered around the body of the dead Buddha, the cat killed a rat which was licking the oil in a lamp. As punishment for having killed a living creature, the cat was excluded from the Zodiac.

One of the most beautiful of Asian legends is that of the Burmese cat. In Burma, the cat was the central figure of a totemistic cult. Priests, known as Kittahs, were believed to migrate, upon their death, into the bodies of cats. To escape the Brahmins, who used to hunt them down and kill them, the Kittahs took refuge in the subterranean temple of Lao Tsun, hidden deep in the mountains of northern Burma, where a venerable priest by the name of Mun Hâ used to live. Throughout his life Mun Hâ contemplated Tsun Kyankse, the sapphire-eyed goddess. By his side, he had an oracle, the cat Sinh, which also kept its gaze fixed upon the statue of the goddess.

One evening, while the temple was under attack from Siamese invaders, Mun Hâ died. The priests saw the cat jump on the head of its dead master and perceived that at that instant, its paws, purified by this contact, had turned white and its eyes blue, as blue as those of the Goddess herself. The cat somehow made the priests understand that they must close the southern portals of the temple, and thanks to this the Siamese troops were repelled. Sinh, however, remained motionless before the statue of the goddess. Seven days after its master, it too died and its soul became one with the goddess.

After another seven days, the Kittah held a conclave to decide who should take Mun Hâ's place. At that moment, a procession of one hundred cats, all looking exactly like Sinh, appeared and formed a circle round the youngest of the priests, thus signifying that he was to be Mun Hâ's successor.

There is a strange custom in Cambodia: at times of drought, people go from house to house, taking a cat with them. At each port of call, the animal is doused with water, and its cries of protest are said to make the rains come. In Tokyo, there is a Temple of the Cats, built only 200 years ago. It contains a curious collection of effigies of cats, made of bronze, china, cloth and other materials. The figurines are tightly bunched, with the cats holding their right forepaws at head height. The temple is surrounded by a cemetery where Buddhists bury their cats. These burial grounds recall the pets' cemeteries one can see in the West, such as the one at Asnières, near Paris.

*   *   *

The cat's entry into Europe was followed by what can only be called a secret war. For centuries after the cat had settled in Europe, Greek spies used to sneak into Egypt to steal cats and, in return, Egyptian agents did their best to recover the animals . . . What a subject for a spy story!

During classical antiquity, however, the cat did not play a particularly prominent role in Europe. True, there are a few mosaics in Pompeii depicting cats devouring birds or mice and, more importantly, some of the Roman legions displayed a cat on their banners—but that is all. It would appear, therefore, that cats were something of a rarity in ancient Greece and Rome, rather as in our own day the mongoose and the coati are rare as pets in Europe.

The Gauls do not seem to have kept cats themselves, but the skeleton of a cat has been found during a dig at the site of a Roman villa at Montmaurin in the Haute-Garonne Department. The cat did not really become established in Western Europe in real strength until the end of the fourth century B.C. Monks from Egypt introduced the cat into a number of regions on the Continent, notably the Rhine Delta. Europe had just been invaded by barbarian hordes, who brought in their wake an undesirable guest—the black rat. Cats were therefore more than welcome. They were used in the fight against the invader and strictly protected by law.

After that, they once again fell into oblivion, as other carnivores were preferred to them, for instance the genet. When the crusaders returned from the Orient, they in their turn brought Egyptian cats with them, and these were once again used to combat the rat plague. They were particularly well received in convents and monasteries: even the monks on Mount Athos, in Greece, who will not normally tolerate the presence of any female being within their precincts, were prepared to put up with she-cats in their monasteries in order to ensure the continuation of the species. Two distinct types were bred by crossing cats newly imported from the East with those already installed in Europe: one with a round head and muscular legs; the other with the slim body and limbs of the Egyptian cat. Unfortunately, the cat was soon struck by misfortune. There can be no doubt that the disasters which befell the animal had their root in the cult of Freya and Holda, two goddesses believed to keep cats as their constant companions. The church prohibited the cult, the disciples of which indulged in strange rites. These included a black mass celebrated by a witch dressed up as a black cat. In fact, it was believed that the cats themselves sometimes organised these rites, and there was a rumour rife among the peasants that on these occasions the cats would utter blasphemies.

As a result, the cat came to be looked upon as a beast of the devil, and the animals were put to the most atrocious tortures including crucifixion. Above all, countless cats were burned alive. At Cahors, for example, in the thirteenth century, the consuls—i.e. the members of the city council—used to set light to what was called the 'Stake of St. John'. This ritual invariably took place on the evening of 23rd June: a pole some 12 m high, surrounded by 500 faggots, was put up in the middle of a crowded square. After a basket containing six cats had been tied to the top of the pole, the First Consul would set the faggots alight with two tapers of yellow wax, each embossed with the city's coat of arms. To the accompaniment of dancing and music, the cats were put to a horrible death. Afterwards the onlookers would share out the charred remains of the faggots, which were supposed to bring good luck.

In Metz, in 1344, thirteen cats were burned alive to stop an epidemic of the mental illness known as 'St. Vitus' dance'. Every year until 1773 this sadistic custom was observed to mark the anniversary of the events of 1344. Louis XI, Henry IV and Louis XIII all watched this and similar spectacles. In several countries, another custom was observed: A number of cats would be placed at the foot of a pole surrounded by a circle of fire. To escape the flames, the animals would scramble up the pole, killing one another in their desperation as they did so. The last cat to survive perished in the flames.

Shrivelled bodies of cats have from time to time been discovered in mediaeval ruins. In the Middle Ages, a live cat would often be immured in buildings under construction. This was believed to strengthen the edifice. In 1747, the Archbishop of Cologne ordered the owners of cats to cut off the animals' ears. Sometimes a curse would be pronounced not only on the cats but also their masters, and people would be hanged or burned at the stake merely because they had kept a cat as a pet.

Another torture sometimes inflicted on cats resulted in a strange tradition which has survived to this day. In Belgium, the custom was to fling cats from the top of cathedral spires. This practice was established in 962 by Baudouin III, Count of Flanders. When he found that the good burghers of Ypres worshipped cats as false idols, the Count ordered them to cease this practice and commanded that a number of cats be thrown to their deaths from the tower of his castle to prove they were not endowed with supernatural powers. Since the fifteenth century, the Cat Festival (*Kattefeest*) has been celebrated each year at Ypres to commemorate this event. Nowadays, the festival is held on the second Sunday in May. On the eve of the festival, a herald proclaims the start of the celebrations from the belfry, and in the early afternoon of the great day itself a procession of more than 1,700 people in fancy dress parades through the town. One of the floats represents the Goddess Freya drawn by two giant cats, while another represents Tibert, the cat which figures as one of the chief characters in the twelfth- and thirteenth-century French collection of stories known as *Roman de Renart*. A third float features Puss-in-Boots, together with the Marquis de Carabas. The Goddess Bastet, too, is there in person. It goes without saying that, since the *Kattefeest* is held in Flanders, giant figures feature in the procession. At six in the evening the official festival jester and his pages appear at the top of the belfry and throw cats among the spectators—but only soft toy ones, of course! This innocent regional custom has been retained to commemorate the torments to which cats were submitted for many centuries.[3]

Despite these tortures, the cat finally gained the place in society that it occupies today. At the end of the seventeenth century, Colbert ordered that two cats should be carried on every French warship. Towards the middle of the eighteenth century, a second variety of rat—the brown or sewer rat—invaded Europe from Central Asia and the cat proved to be the best defence against this new invader.

Thereafter, its place in society was never again contested. In the meantime, the Europeans had introduced the cat into America.

Even in its darkest hours, the cat had enjoyed the friendship of powerful and influential men such as Richelieu and Montaigne. To Baudelaire, cats were 'Great Sphinxes stretched out in noble attitudes sunk in the depths of solitude'.

Anatole France saw in his cat Hamilcar 'a sleepy prince from the city of books' combining 'the formidable aspect of a Tartar warrior with the ponderous grace of an Oriental lady'. More recently, Colette and Léautaud professed themselves devoted friends and admirers of cats. Colette describes most affectionately her cat's 'paw with its claws and its underneath coloured a delicate pink and black, rather like a rose with its thorns'. Paul Léautaud was never without anything up to forty-five cats at a time! He says in his *Chronique dramatique*: 'When I appear, there is nothing else for it—they all gather around me and clamber on my knees and shoulders, showering me with signs of affection.'

There have been many other prominent cat lovers. In his book *Une Chatte comme les autres*, René-Pierre Audras lists a whole number of them. He tells us that Pope Leo XII invariably used to conceal a kitten in the folds of his *soutane*. Charles Dickens would go on writing of an evening until such time as his cat put out the candle with its paw. Sir Walter Scott was deeply grieved by the death of his cat, and innumerable authors, from Mallarmé to Claude Farrère, were quite unable to work unless their cat was there on their writing desk.

We thus get a picture very different from the unflattering image of the cat which the writers of a more distant past used to paint: thus, Tibert in the *Roman de Renart*, is a rascal. Perrault's Puss in Boots, on the other hand, was a much more attractive character. Cats have also inspired many painters: Courbet featured a white cat in his *L'atelier du peintre* and Manet a black one in his painting *L'Olympia*. There are also paintings of cats by Delacroix, Géricault, Fujita and Picasso. When his cat Patrocles died, Ingres cancelled all his engagements and shut himself up in his room for a whole day and night.

Countless politicians are known to have been cat lovers—Lincoln and Doumergue, Clemenceau and Poincaré, Blum and Churchill. Of the many scientists who loved cats, suffice it to mention Fauré, Einstein and Dr. Schweitzer.

*   *   *

One of the most attractive breeds is the French Chartreux, with its slate-grey coat and yellow eyes. Thanks to a recent study of Jean Simonnet, we can trace the history of the breed. According to Simonnet, a poem by du Bellay[4] gives the first authentic description of this breed. Du Bellay mentions among other things that his beloved Belaud gave short shrift to many a rat, and it is a fact that the Chartreux is an excellent hunter.

The name of Chartreux was, as far as we know, first used in 1766 by Buffon and was included three years later in the *Dictionnaire raisonné et universal des animaux*. According to this work, it was only in Paris that the breed was known as '*Chartreux*', so we are dealing here with a truly Parisian cat. But how did the monks of the *Grande Chartreuse* monastery come to be mixed up in this story? Their habit was never the greyish-blue colour of our animal, nor have they ever bred one particular breed of cats. By way of an explanation Jean Simonnet suggests that the cats must at some time in the past have lived in one of the several other monasteries also known as '*Chartreuse*'—perhaps in the one which occupied the grounds of the present-day *Jardin du Luxembourg* in Paris.

The long-haired Persian or Angora cat was introduced into Italy in 1626 by a Roman gentleman by the name of Pietro di Valle, on his return from Persia. Six years later, a member of the 'Parliament of Aix', Nicolas Fabri de Peirex, brought the breed to France.

Two centuries later, in 1884, the Siamese—the royal cat of the Court of Thailand—made its first appearance in Europe. Specimens of the breed were brought to London by a Mrs. Veley, sister of the British Consul General in Bangkok. Later still, Auguste Pavie, formerly French Resident in Siam, made a present of several Siamese cats to—of all people—the board of the *Jardin des Plantes* botanical gardens in Paris.

Since then several other breeds have been introduced into Europe: the brownish-russet Abyssinian, whose configuration recalls the ancient Egyptian cat, was brought to England in 1866. The Burmese cat—the subject of the beautiful legend mentioned earlier in this chapter—was introduced into Europe at about 1918.

The Isle of Man is renowned for its tailless cat, which incidentally, has another peculiar trait—its long, hare-like hind legs. An amusing legend is supposed to explain how the breed acquired these two characteristics:

To scare off the Irish invaders who time and again ravaged the island, the local people decided to make themselves look more imposing by tying cat's tails to their helmets. This, of course, meant that countless cats were killed. To save her litter, a mother-cat about to give birth escaped into the hills and, as soon as her kittens were born, bit off their tails. When they had grown a little bigger, the kittens found that to get down a slope it was easier to slide on their hind quarters than to run. This caused their hind legs to grow longer and their hind quarters rounder than those of any other cat. We are told that this story greatly amused Lamarck, the French naturalist, who always emphasised the influence of environmental factors on inherited characteristics.

When the members of the litter returned to the lowlands, they saw that all the other cats had been killed. So, when these kittens became cats and had their own litters, they, in their turn, bit off their kittens' tails, and after a few generations, the young were born without tails. And so it came about that Manx cats have no tails.

*   *   *

Cats figure in a great many legends, both in Europe and in other parts of the world. We are told that at Bouxwiller, Alsace, there is a cat which can enter and leave a house by walking clean through a brick wall which opens up for him. In the Chateau de Combourg, in Brittany, the young Chateaubriand is said to have observed the wooden leg of a dead count wandering through the countryside on its own, accompanied only by a black cat. It is true that the skeleton of a cat has been found in one of the chateau's towers, which is now known as 'Cat Tower'. In the Vosges mountains people used to think that if someone should surreptitiously slip the leg of a black cat into a hunter's game bag, this would affect his aim. Many legends are told in Scotland, India and Japan of women being changed into cats, and we shall return to these stories later.

Superstitions about cats abound among seafaring folk. Scottish seamen believe that a storm is bound to follow if a cat should scratch a table leg. The Slav peoples are convinced that during a storm cats are possessed by demons. In Ireland, at the approach of a storm, people would place a metal jug over their cats. This was supposed to force the animals to make the storm abate by using their supernatural powers. Japanese sailors used to believe that cats with coats of three colours have the power to calm a storm.

In European folklore the cat symbolises eternity, and in some countries it is supposed to have nine lives. The figure nine is mystical—the trinity of trinities (3 × 3). A cat can in fact fall from a great height without getting killed, and this has undoubtedly contributed to the birth of the legend about cats being immortal. Moslems believe that the Prophet touched a cat's spine and thus enabled it to avoid falling on its back.

In Scotland, neolithic stones are known as 'Cat's stones', and in Kent there is a cromlech[5] which goes by the name of 'Kit's Coty House'. There is clearly a link between the supposed immortality of cats and the fact that these stones are regarded as symbols of indestructibility. In several regions of Europe and Africa it is thought to be unlucky to maltreat a cat, while in ancient Egypt, as we have said, it was a crime to kill a cat.

*   *   *

In many languages (Greek, Latin, Arabic, French, German, English, Russian) the word for cat is derived from the common Indo-European root *ghad*, which stands for the verb 'to catch'. In the Jewish Talmud the word for cat is 'that which catches'. To the Chinese Buddhists, a cat crouching immobile before pouncing on its quarry was a symbol of meditation.

In our own time, the only real task performed by cats is to hunt mice and other rodents, and even this aspect is tending to vanish, for the cat has largely become a pet. In Paraguay, however, cats are used to hunt the rattlesnake.

A Russian legend pays tribute to the cat's skill as a hunter: a dog and a cat were on guard at the Gates of Paradise when Lucifer tried to gain entry disguised as a mouse. The dog was ready to let him pass but the cat pounced on the mouse. Another legend has it that God created the cat and Satan the mouse. The latter tried to destroy the living world by gnawing at the hull of Noah's Ark. Fortunately, the cat killed the mouse before much harm was done. In some regions, the cat is credited with being able to hunt and kill much larger quarry. Various West African tribes explain the eclipse of the moon by saying that from time to time the cat—which they equate with the sun—swallows the moon.

There are many other things the cat is supposed to symbolise. In his standard work *The Cult of the Cat*, P. Dale-Green lists, in particular: motherhood, virginity and freedom. As we have said, the cat's strong maternal instinct made a deep impression on the ancient Egyptians. A Polish folk tale tells of a cat which was weeping because its young had fallen into a river. A compassionate willow tree saved them by lowering its branches into the water. Hence, to this day, we call the flowers of this tree 'Pussy Willows'.

In many parts of the world the cat is associated with the fertility of the soil and it consequently plays a part in numerous country customs. In Egypt, a ceremony was held each year to commemorate the death of the cat-god Osiris. Later, in Europe, Osiris was assimilated into the figure of the cat pure and simple, and the latter came to be worshipped as the spirit of grain. Thus, the tradition was born of placing a cat in the last sheaf of corn at harvest time. There the poor beast was left to be killed by the threshing flails. In the Vosges, the popular name for wheat used to be *le chat*.

At Amiens, the good folk of the town used to sacrifice a cat to ensure an abundant harvest the following year, and at harvest time people would stop their work to see the animal being put to death. In China, special thanksgiving ceremonies were common to mark the end of the harvest at which the cat would be honoured for having kept down the rodents harmful to the crop. The Indonesians believe that cats can be made to bring rain: all you have to do is to dip a cat in a pool of water! In some European countries, a cat washing behind the ears is thought to bring rain!

The cat's cleanliness was the cause of its becoming a symbol of virginity. The theme was taken up by Christianity, and there is a legend of a female cat being placed in the manger at Bethlehem. There is a picture by Leonardo da Vinci showing the Virgin with a cat. In many versions of the famous folk tale of which she is the heroine, Cinderella is described as owning a cat. In the Danish version, a tom cat asks Cinders for a bowl of milk. Having drunk it, he grows and sheds his fur to turn into a Prince Charming who marries the heroine.

Because of its independence and refusal to submit to servitude, the cat also became a symbol of freedom. As we have said, in ancient Rome some of the legions—and more especially those charged with defending the liberty of the State—sported pictures of cats on their banners. The theme of the cat as a symbol of freedom was to be echoed later in Switzerland, the Netherlands and France. Liberty, as pictured in the statue put up in its honour by the First French Republic, had a cat at its feet. A large tom cat sitting at the feet of Liberty is also featured in a painting by Prud'hon.

Faith in the cat's healing powers was not confined to Egypt. In Europe it was thought that rheumatic inflammations could be cured by massaging the affected joint with cat's fur. In other parts of the world the belief is widespread that cats' fur can cure blindness. It is the cat's tail, in particular, that is thought to help in this respect, and in Britain there is a popular belief that you should treat a stye by rubbing the eyelid affected with a cat's tail.

In all these customs and beliefs the cat appears as a useful and attractive figure. However, there is another side to the story—a side which has caused the animals to suffer atrocious tortures in the Middle Ages. As against the white cat, which was thought to bring good fortune, there was the malevolent black cat, with the evil eye. Like all the other superstitions we have mentioned, there is an explanation for this. Cats like to be out and about at night, and their swift, silent movements seem threatening to some people, to whom the animal seems the very embodiment of the mystery of the night and of darkness. There is, in fact, an even more specific reason for the fact that black cats are associated with this particular belief: according to an old legend, the Goddess of Darkness, Diana, existed before the world had been created. Later, she split into a male half, which was light, and a female half, which was dark. The male half became Diana's brother, Lucifer (from *lux*, light). Diana fell in love with Lucifer, who rejected her. Having become aware that Lucifer owned a cat, she persuaded the animal to change places with her. Thus it came to pass that Diana bore Lucifer a daughter, Aradia, who became the world's first witch. Diana sent Aradia into the world, where she taught the humans the art of black magic. This could well be one explanation of the age-old belief that there is a link between the cat and witchcraft.

*   *   *

The cat is mentioned in many proverbs. The ancient French saying about a scalded cat fearing even cold water,[6] which dates from the Middle Ages, is paralleled by an Arab proverb: 'A cat that has been

bitten by a snake is frightened at the sight of a rope.' The proverb
'When the cat is away the mice will play' exists in French, Italian,
English, Spanish, Portuguese and Dutch. In Madagascar, the same
idea is expressed in somewhat different words: 'The rat will not
budge so long as he can see the gleam of the cat's eyes.'

[1] The best effigies of cats are those to be found on the graves of the sculptors
Apuki and Nebamun at Thebes, which date from the reign of Amenophis III, and at
the Temple of Medinat-Abu.

[2] Supreme state to which Buddhists aspire.

[3] Until the end of the last century, so-called 'cats' concerts' used to be customary
at fairs: the unfortunate animals were enclosed in boxes and the owner would pull
their tails to make them miaow.

[4] French sixteenth-century poet (tr.).

[5] Megalithic monument consisting of a circle of menhirs (upright stones, up to 20
metres high).

[6] Chat échaudé craint l'eau froide.

CHAPTER THREE

Animals as Man's Helpers in Hunting and Fishing

AS WE have seen, at the beginning the main role of the cat and the dog was to help man hunt, but now they have become, first and foremost, domestic pets.

In the course of man's evolution, many other species were trained to catch game. We have referred, in this context, to the small beasts of prey which were used to hunt rodents before the cat was finally domesticated in sufficient numbers. The Egyptians used the mongoose to keep down rodents, and the animal is still employed in India to hunt snakes. The Greeks and the Romans are said to have trained the marten, and possibly also the polecat and stoat, to help them hunt. Contrary, however, to some accounts, they did not tame the weasel, which has always resisted domestication.

In the Middle Ages, the genet was highly popular. This small wild animal, which still survives in central and southern France, used to be kept by noblemen in their castles, while the marten was used by farmers. Together with other domesticated animals, the genet is featured on a famous fifteenth-century French tapestry known as *Dame à la Licorne* (Lady with Unicorn). After the Battle of Poitiers (732 or 733), Charles Martel went so far as to create an Order of the Genet in recognition of the gallantry shown by his comrades in arms.

The only small carnivore which continues to serve man to this day is the ferret. There has been some controversy about the origin of this animal, which is generally regarded as a more or less degenerate semi-albino mutant of the polecat. It certainly has red eyes—the typical mark of an albino. The ferret cross-breeds readily with the true polecat; the hybrid has a darker coat.

There do not seem to be any ferrets in the wild state on the Continent of Europe, though there have been reports of some having been seen in Sardinia and Sicily. It is certainly true that polecat–ferret hybrids which have managed to escape can survive for some considerable time living wild.

A French popular saying goes: 'He runs, he runs, the ferret, the ferret of the beautiful forest.' He has, in fact, been running so fast that scientists have had a good deal of trouble tracing his origins. His home seems to have been North Africa, the 'Libya' of the ancients, and he is said to have been introduced into Europe from that region. Pliny the Elder reports that the people of the Balearic Islands asked the Emperor Augustus to give them ferrets with which to hunt the rabbits that were destroying their crops, and this indeed is the purpose for which the ferret is used by man to this day. The little beast is taken in a sack or a box to the rabbit's burrow and released into it, all exits but one being blocked. The rabbits scurry out by the one available exit and are then, of course, at the hunter's mercy. The ferret, threading its way through the dark subterranean tunnels, reminds people of a thief in the night, and it is to this that he owes his name, for *fur* means thief in Latin.

The famous writer and naturalist Louis Pergaud tells of a polecat, a weasel, a common marten and a stone-marten who have decided to put an end to the life of the ferret Yellowfur. To them, Yellowfur is nothing but a traitor who has allowed man to turn him into a slave and who competes with the wild animals for food. One day, during a hunt, the polecat takes him by surprise and kills him.

*　　*　　*

The fastest member of the cat family, the cheetah, was highly fashionable in the Middle Ages. In the thirteenth century, the German Emperor Frederick II owned several 'leoparderies', which were in fact enclosures where not leopards but cheetahs were kept. These animals are featured in the famous tapestry of Queen Mathilde as well as in the one known as the 'Lady with Unicorn', and are also depicted in the famous Book of Hours *Très Riches Heures du duc de Berry*. During the Renaissance the cheetah was much in vogue in Italy. In 1418, the Prince of Achaea presented to Mary of Burgundy a cheetah with a silver collar, a lead of fringed silk and a green velvet coat.

However, it was in Egypt, Persia and India that the cheetah was most highly prized as a hunting animal. In the last of these countries, hunting with the aid of a cheetah was popular until quite recently. The beast was blindfolded before being taken to the place of the hunt. The blindfold was only removed when the quarry was in sight, and then the cheetah would pounce. In the sixteenth century, we are told, the Emperor Akbar owned no fewer than 1,000 cheetahs trained for antelope hunting. The use of the cheetah as an aid to man in hunting has come to an end in India, for the very good reason that the animal is now probably extinct there. In recent years, the cheetah has become something of a plaything among a handful of the 'trendy' rich, and some cheetahs have in fact been seen being taken for a walk in the streets of Paris. However, the cheetah is just about the last animal that should be kept captive in a house or an apartment, and the practice is greatly to be deplored.

In India, another member of the cat family, the caracal—a sort of Afro-Asian lynx—is used for hunting pigeons. If Marco Polo is to be believed, a beast of prey of much more impressive size—the tiger—was also used for hunting. The famous Venetian explorer claims to have seen in the park of the Mongol Ruler Kublai Khan, tigers trained to hunt boar, stags, wild buffalo, etc. Marco Polo—who tells us the tigers were taken to the hunt in cages carried on carts and let loose when the game was in sight—calls the beasts 'lions', but from his description ('a splendid coat, striped black, white and red') there can be no doubt about the animal he had in mind. Much earlier, the Roman Emperor Heliogabalus drove through Rome in a chariot drawn by tigers.

*   *   *

Above all, however, it was birds of prey which were used for hunting—large falcons such as the Saker, the Lanner and the Peregrine being the most highly prized. The splendid Arctic Gyr, with his white plumage, was much sought after, and every year a Danish ship would leave for the Far North in search of these birds. In Central Asia the Golden Eagle was used for fox hunting.

In addition to these high-flying birds, some low-flying ones were in use for hunting, such as the Sparrow Hawk and the Goshawk. Night birds, too, were trained for hunting—the Eagle Owl, for instance, and men also used ravens and even shrikes for this purpose—the latter for hunting somewhat humbler prey—sparrows. Louis XIII was known to have used shrikes to hunt sparrows in his gardens at the Palais du Louvre.

However, falcons were used for hunting at a much earlier date—by the ancient Greeks—and in the distant past the birds were also employed for hunting in India and Persia. The art of falconry was very widespread in Europe between the sixth and seventeenth centuries. In our own time, it has survived above all in the Middle East. Some oil sheikhs own Cadillac *coupés* from which they release the birds.

The extraordinary skill which has been shown in developing the art of falconry since the Middle Ages has been described by Prof. Pierre P. Grassé,[1] and treatises have been written on this subject by many other authors, including the German Emperor Frederick II. The first step is to teach the bird how to remain still while hooded, perched on the gloved hand of its master. The bird's feet are tied by means of leather thongs. The falconer then 'unhoods' the bird and offers him a piece of meat.

Next, the bird is taken out into the open and put down on the ground. The hood is once again taken off and the bird shown a piece of meat. It is then taught to pick its meat from its master's hand. The third stage of the bird's training goes as follows: The falcon is shown the lure—a leather pad to which a piece of carcass of the quarry the bird is being taught to hunt is attached. The bird is taught to grab the meat while the lure is swung round and round at the end of a line. Having seized the meat, the falcon must be trained to return to hand. It is now almost ready for hunting other birds, i.e. the falconer is almost ready to 'fly' his bird. The females were used to hunt heron; the male or tiercel, being smaller than the female, had to make do with partridge, quail or pigeon. To obtain the best results, the falconer uses a wide range of methods to control his bird: rewards, bait, whistle calls, and so forth.[2]

*   *   *

Other birds are used for fishing, above all the cormorant, which is greatly prized for this purpose in China and Japan. The fisherman takes a few birds with him in a boat and when he has arrived on station puts one of the birds down on the water, after first placing a ring round its neck. The bird will dive at a fish, but—because of the ring—cannot, of course, swallow it. The fisherman then retrieves the catch with a net and, after rewarding the bird with a few mouthfuls of food, lets him fly off again to catch more fish. The fishermen on Lake Dojran in Yugoslavia also make use of birds, but in a different manner. They build rows of tanks made of reeds and submerge them in the lake. As soon as the fish have entered the first of the tanks through a hole that has been left open, the tank is closed and diving birds whose wings have been clipped (such as mergansers, grebes and cormorants) are put into the tank. To escape the birds, the fish move into the adjoining tank, using openings too small for the birds to negotiate. The process is repeated from tank to tank, until the fish have all been gathered in the last and smallest tank, from which they are lifted.

An even more extraordinary helpmate of the fishermen is a sea fish—the remora. Measuring about 40 cm it is equipped with a sucking plate at the top of its head, consisting of some twenty horizontal blades which move in parallel rather like a Venetian blind. The sucking plate adheres to any object it touches—it could be a shark, a tortoise, a whale or a dolphin, or even a ship, which will then give the remora a free ride.

The adhesive power of the remora, though very considerable, has been greatly exaggerated. According to Pliny the Elder, a number of remora fish decided the outcome of the battle of Actium by stopping Mark Anthony's ship! In Madagascar, in the Caribbean and other parts of the world the remora is tied to a line and let loose against other fish, which he takes back to his master. One of Christopher Columbus' crew claimed as early as 1504 to have seen American Indians catching sea turtles with the aid of a remora.

Otters, too, have been used for fishing, both in Europe and India.

These were, however, only sporadic experiments which have never been followed up.

¹ *Traité de Zoologie*, vol. XV, p. 1119, ed. Masson.

² Nowadays a new use has been found for falcons: they are employed at airports to chase away flocks of starlings, which are a hazard to aircraft.

CHAPTER FOUR

Cattle

CATTLE ARE without a doubt one of the most important domesticated species in the modern world, and are also among those tamed earliest. According to recent discoveries, the domestication of cattle appears to have begun at roughly the same time at the two extremes of Asia—to be more exact, Palestine[1] and Thailand.

In the first of these regions, very precise data have been collected by Pierre du Cos, a member of the staff of a French research institute which specialises in the ecology of prehistoric man, the Centre de recherches d'écologie et de préhistoire, at St. André-de-Cruzières (Ardèche). The domestication of cattle began in Palestine towards the end of the seventh millenium B.C.[2] Bone remains found at Hagoshrim, near Lake Huleh (Israel), are undoubtedly those of domestic cattle. This is evident from the age spread of the specimens discovered. Let us try to be more precise: in any group of wild animals, the newborn will, in the nature of things, outnumber all the rest. The older age groups will progressively decrease in number as mortality rises due to various causes. At the prehistoric site near Lake Huleh, however, bones of five-year-old animals are the most numerous. This means that mortality was greatest among animals of that age—a fact for which there can be only one explanation: the local people killed their cattle at the age of five, i.e. after they had attained sexual maturity; in other words, the breeders delayed killing their animals until the latter had produced offspring.

Let us speculate a little about the methods used in Palestine to domesticate cattle. There can hardly be any doubt that the first cereal crops to be grown attracted wild cattle from far and wide. This must have presented man with an opportunity to catch and raise calves. From 3200 B.C. onward, cattle were used in the Middle East as draught animals to help man cultivate his fields, as we can see from a specimen of stoneware found in Mesopotamia.

The second centre of the domestication of cattle—and at approximately the same time as the one in Palestine—was Nok Nok Tha, in Thailand. The bones of cattle found at this site are remarkable for their weight—which proves that the animals were well nourished and hence probably domesticated. This site was inhabited between 5000 and 3500 B.C. by a people who worked bronze and grew rice. It is therefore hardly surprising that they should also have kept domestic cattle.

But what, exactly, is the ancestry of the cattle of our own day? There can be no doubt that our cattle are descended from a wild ancestor, but which one? The Aurochs (*Bos primigenius*) seems to have been the ancestor of most of the present-day breeds, though the Highland shorthorn (*Bos longifrons*), which had an elongated face, may have contributed to the emergence of some of the modern breeds. The Aurochs was a big beast with lyre-shaped horns, standing between 1.80 and 2 metres high at the shoulder. The coat of the bull was black, while that of the cow was red. Prehistoric man was well acquainted with this animal, and numerous rock paintings of it have been found, notably at Lascaux. The species was still fairly well established at the time of classical antiquity and played an important part in the Mesopotamian and Cretan civilisations. There is a description of it in Julius Caesar's *Gallic Wars*.

The breeds common in the Camargue, Corsica and Spain have retained most of the characteristics of the Aurochs except for size, being much smaller. In 1931, Lutz Heck, a German zoologist, conceived the idea of 'reconstructing' the Aurochs on the basis of these breeds. He obtained, by means of skilful selection, bulls whose appearance was very similar to that of the Aurochs. Although the war interrupted this promising work, a number of specimens were fortunately saved and their progeny can be seen in a nature park at Han-sur-Lesse, in Belgium. This beast might be called the 'neo-Aurochs'.

From the Middle East, several waves of cattle entered Africa via the Suez Isthmus with the pastoral people who owned them. It is these animals which are featured on the rock paintings in the Tassili Mountains in the Sahara.

The history of domestic cattle can be traced with particular accuracy in Britain. The first breed that lived in the British Isles was the Highland shorthorn (*Bos longifrons*). Subsequently, the Romans introduced white cattle into Britain. Descendants of these massive beasts can be seen to this day in the parks at Chillingham and Chartley, where they live in the wild state. The Anglo-Saxons then brought a red-coated breed into Britain and, finally, the Danes introduced a dark brown breed which had the unusual characteristic of being hornless.

*   *   *

The bull has throughout history played an immensely important part in the traditions and religious rites of most civilisations. Its strength and dignity have never failed to inspire both admiration and fear in people.

Paintings of bulls have been found at prehistoric sites at Sialk, in Iran, and at a neolithic site at Mariupol, near the Azov Sea, while figurines of bulls have been discovered in a Scythian burial ground of the third millennium, at Maikop.

In the Indus Basin, the rock paintings of the Mohenjo-daro and Harappa civilisation show bull-like animals with, apparently, only a single horn which points forward. These would therefore seem to be unicorns. In fact, however, the other horn may be hidden by the one which is visible. The paintings show a strange object, which may be a ritual vessel—possibly an incense-burner—standing in front of each of these bulls. In the Hindu religion the animals themselves became one with Nandi, the emblem of the God Shiva, and the Sanscrit word for bull also means 'god' or 'prince'. Moreover, in the *Veda*, the ancient Hindu scripture, the bull is associated with Heaven. In the *Atharvaveda*, a record of ceremonial magic, the God Shiva says: 'My roar is like that of a bull booming forth, thunderlike, across the sky.'

In Mesopotamia, the most important Sumerian divinity was the god-bull Enlil. The life-giving floods of the rivers Tigris and Euphrates were believed to be the result of the union of Enlil with Ninlil, a cow whose image merged with that of the mother-goddess. The Sumerian kings wore a horned helmet, which symbolised the godlike nature of royalty. The Aurochs, whose habitat at that time was the Middle East, was greatly feared by the people of Mesopotamia, if the following Sumerian proverb is anything to go by: 'I have escaped a wild bull only to meet a wild cow.'

To the peoples of the ancient East, the bull symbolised the forces of procreation. In the Chaldean Zodiac, the symbol of the bull also stood for the Sun and for courage. In Syria, too, the bull was associated with the Sun, while in Mesopotamia it symbolised justice. In the latter region, the portico at Ishtar, built by King Nebuchad-nezzar in honour of the Great Lord Marduk, is covered with bas-reliefs on which effigies of dragons alternate with those of bulls. These bulls are also clearly representations of the Aurochs. In a cuneiform inscription, the animal was called *rimi* by the monarch himself, and it is repeatedly referred to as *re'em* in the Bible. According to B. Heuvelmans, a King, who was no doubt Teglath-Phalasar I (1115–1093 B.C.), is described, on an Assyrian obelisk, as 'destroyer of the savage *rimi*, whom he slew at the foot of the Lebanon'. The Assyrians made effigies of winged bulls, examples of which can be seen in the Louvre.

Some of the effigies of bulls by Mesopotamian artists are particularly remarkable. A lapis-lazuli cylinder found at Warka, dating from the third millennium, shows a bull being carried on a ship, with farming implements lashed to his back. Bulls are often pictured side by side with lions, birds or ears of corn. Some of the bulls' heads produced by these artists are notable for their life-like appearance, and the accuracy and strength of the Mesopotamian bull effigies is extraordinary.

The Egypt of the Pharaohs worshipped three bulls: Bukhis, who was always shown as being white with a black head; Mnevis, who had a black coat sprinkled with ears of corn; and above all Apis, who was venerated at Memphis and was black with white spots. He had a triangle on his forehead and carried a crescent or an eagle with spread wings on his back. Apis was believed to be an incarnation of Râ, the God of the Sun. It should be noted in this connection that the cult of Apis was not intended to honour the entire species but one individual bull, chosen for the characteristics of his coat. This animal would be kept in seclusion for forty days and fattened by the priests of the cult. Apart from the priests, only women were allowed to see the bull.

Apis would then be taken to Memphis in a sacred ship. In the city, a sumptuous apartment, consisting of several rooms furnished with beds, was set aside for his use in the temple of Ptah. Every one of his movements was thought to be endowed with a special significance. Animals which reached the age of twenty-five years may have been drowned in a fountain dedicated to the Sun; however, we are not certain of this. On the anniversary of the bull's arrival at the temple a magnificent festival was held, and on his death official mourning was observed for sixty days. The animal would then be mummified and the body placed in a sarcophagus. The chief priest would thereupon begin the search for a new Apis—a bull with the same markings.

In Egypt, cattle intended for slaughter were caught by means of a lasso. The procedure must have resembled a modern rodeo. During the New Empire, zebu replaced the bull, and in the Middle Ages the domestic buffalo was introduced into Egypt. We shall have occasion to discuss these two animals later.

From Egypt, the cult of the bull spread across Africa as far as present-day Natal. In our own day, the Dinka and Nuer peoples of the Sudan still shape the horns of their bulls the way the ancient Egyptians used to do: i.e. one horn is made to point forward and the other backward.[3] The Venda tribesmen in the Transvaal always have one black bull, whom they call 'Grandfather' and who, to them, embodies the spirits of their ancestors. Cattle also have an important place in East African poetry. To the Herero, cattle are sacred. Their chief is always buried in an ox skin and himself turns into the spirit of an ox. Cattle dung and urine play a part in the religious ceremonial of these people.

The bull was the only animal venerated as a god by the Hittites, who saw in him the God of Tempests. In the religion of the Canaanites, the chief god, the father of Baal, was the 'Bull God'. Baal himself was horned and his symbol was the bull.

*   *   *

According to Aegean mythology, Pasiphae, wife of King Minos, fell in love with a bull who had emerged from the waves. Of this union the Minotaur was born, a bloodthirsty monster with the body of a man and the head of a bull. He was killed by Theseus. In Persian legend, too, the hero Mithras is said to have killed a bull. The legend of the Minotaur shows how fascinated the Cretans were by this animal. In fact, the art of bull fighting comes from ancient Crete, and it is the redoubtable Aurochs which the island's inhabitants used to fight. Certain aspects of the description of the Minotaur which, according to legend, was vanquished by Hercules, recall the Aurochs.

As we can see from the frescoes of Knossos and the gold bowls of Vaphio, the Cretans fought these animals, the latter bearing down on them at full speed. The bullfighter would at the last moment execute a dangerous leap over the running bull or, alternatively, he might grab him by the horns and jump on his back. The bullfighter would sometimes kill the animal by wringing its neck, particularly if it was young. These 'corridas' would occasionally end with the animal being sacrificed to the Minoan mother-goddess. Such scenes are, at any rate, depicted on Mycenean carved stones. A painting found on a sarcophagus at Hagia Triada pictures such a ritual sacrifice. It seems that the bull's blood was collected in a vessel while a priestess offered up libations at an altar. There would appear to be a connection between this ritual and the cult of the mother-goddess. It may even be that the receptacle had no bottom so that the blood would pour through on to the ground to join mother-earth. At the Cretan spring festivals, the bull symbolised nature's powers of regeneration. The reader may recall that we encountered the same theme in connection with the Middle East.

In the work 'Heracles the Lion-killer', which is attributed to Theocritus, the bulls of Augias, sacred to the Sun, are described as follows: 'Their coat was white as a swan and they stood out among all animals . . . Among them the great Phaethon was distinguished by his strength, his power and his pride, and all the herdsmen compared him to a star for, as he walked with the other bulls, all eyes were upon him.'

In his *Crito,* Plato recounts that the kings of Atlantis would fall upon a group of bulls let loose in a sacred enclosure and, having caught one of them, would cut his throat and sprinkle themselves with his blood.

In ancient Greece and Rome, the spectacle of bullfighting was made even more thrilling by the addition of a new feature: men on horseback would seize the animal by the horns and bring it down. After the publication of Julius Caesar's *Gallic Wars* the Aurochs was much sought after in Rome for circus acts. Caesar, as the reader may recall, in fact described the Aurochs he had seen in the Hercynian Forest. The Roman spectacle of the *tauria* was undoubtedly associated with the cult of Neptune, father of Theseus. Bulls were also sacrificed to the Iranian Goddess Anahita, subsequently identified with Cybele, and from the fourth century onward that cult was linked with the worship of Mithras.

Another Roman ceremony—described by Prudentius—was the *taurobolium*: a bull decorated with flowers was put to death above a pit in which the initiate would be waiting to be drenched in the animal's blood to the cheering of the crowd. This strange ritual is perhaps at the root of the ceremony of the fatted ox, which survived in Europe until quite recently.[4] Occasionally an altar would be put up to commemorate a *taurobolium*. An example of such a structure has been preserved at Perigueux. So important was the *taurobolium* that it provided strong competition to Christianity during its early stages.

Later the cult of the bull spread to Western and Northern Europe. The Celts would brandish emblems bearing the effigy of a bull. Their bull god was associated in their eyes with the sky, the oak tree and the tempest (they shared the latter belief with the Hittites). The Celtic cult of the bull eventually spread to Scandinavia, and the Vikings, like the Celts and the Sumerians, wore horned helmets. In the Edda sagas, the God Thor devours a whole bull. The cult also reached Britain, where bullfights were organised, with the animals representing rival groups. Bull Rock, near Loch Lomond, commemorates the fight between the black bull of Scotland and the red bull of England.

*   *   *

Step by step, the modern *corridas*, devoid of all religious associations, developed. They existed among the Visigoths at the beginning of the Middle Ages, but did not become widespread in Spain until the sixteenth century. Charles V organised a *corrida* to mark the birth of his son, the future Philip II. In the eighteenth century, dogs played a part in the Spanish *corridas*. In those days, the matadors were still considered to be low class, rather like the *bestiarii* of ancient Rome, and it was only later that they became heroes.

In our own days, bullfighting can take various forms. In Portugal, the points of the bull's horns are covered with leather and it is forbidden to kill the animal. In France, too, the bull may not be killed, to avoid protests from the animal protection societies. The rodeos, popular in North America, are strongly reminiscent of the games once popular in ancient Crete.

On the island of Bali, in Indonesia, games which recall the ancient Cretan sacrifices are still held. In the Tamil regions of India, games are organised which closely resemble a spectacle popular in the Landes region of south-western France: the object is to get hold of a rag tied to the bull's horns. According to J. Duchaussoy, 'the belief that fertility is the gift of a heavenly bull still survives in the Basque country festival of the *Toro de fuego*, to the head of which a large number of fireworks are fastened; people believe that the size of the forthcoming harvest will be in proportion to the height reached by the sparks which fly off the head of the fire bull'. Just like dogs and pigs, bulls used to have to 'stand trial' for attacking children. The bull theme lives on in modern art and literature. As examples we need merely cite Picasso's *Guernica*—in which the bull symbolises war—and Montherlant's *Les Bestiaires*.

There are several instances of the calf and the cow, rather than the bull, figuring in folklore and mythology. The Bible tells us that while Moses was on Mount Sinai, the Jews, at the instigation of Aaron, made a Golden Calf and worshipped it. Moses, full of anger, turned the idol to dust. The Golden Calf also features in French folklore, especially in the Périgord region, where, according to the peasants, the Golden Calf was kept in the vaults of a castle and could be glimpsed through a hole in an iron trapdoor.

The cow as a symbol appears in the Middle East and India. In the former, the mother-goddess was identified with the cow. Both in Egypt, at the end of the predynastic period, and in the Euphrates region, this goddess, known as Hathor, was represented in various forms: either as a female deity with the disc of the sun adorning her head, flanked by the horns of a bull or a cow, or as a cow displaying between her horns the disc of the sun flanked by two feathers. Hathor was at one and the same time the mother, the wife and the wet-nurse of Horus. The cult of the cow goddess spread to Sinai, Nubia and Syria. At al-Obeid, in Mesopotamia, the mother-goddess Nin-Khursag was also represented as a cow and formed part of a totemistic cult. Her wedding with the Moon God was celebrated there each year. In Greek mythology, Io, Princess of Argos, was changed into a heifer by Zeus.

*   *   *

The cow plays a fundamental part in the traditions of India. We have asked an expert on that country, M. Louis Marcel Gauthier, to describe for us the role of the cow in Indian life. Here is his reply:

In a statement in which he proclaimed himself an orthodox Hindu, Gandhi included this ardent profession of faith:

> The most characteristic feature of Hinduism is the reverence with which it treats the cow. To protect the cow seems to me one of the most admirable manifestations of human progress. To me, the cow is the embodiment of the whole infra-human world; she enables the believer to grasp his unity with all that lives. It seems to me a self-evident truth that the cow is a natural choice as a symbol of that unity . . . The cow is a poem of compassion . . . To protect her is to protect all the dumb creatures of God's creation.[5]

Gandhi had in fact spent part of his life outside India and maintained close relations with Western thinkers, and some critics have discerned in his religious fervour, which he extended to all lower creatures, influences which are not specifically Indian. For example, the impact on him of Tolstoy's thinking is clear—Tolstoy, with whom the Mahatma, according to his own testimony, had certain affinities. However, as regards man's specific relationship with the cow as such, did Gandhi keep strictly to Brahmanic tradition?

> Light-skinned cows can be seen roaming at will through most of India's towns, and the Hindus bow reverently to any that may happen to cross their

path. Some people perform acts of worship by treating cows to delicacies they are known to be fond of.
Wealthy people set aside special buildings as retire-
ment homes for old or sick cows. On certain holy
days, cows are marched down to the river in procession to bathe, their heads painted saffron and
vermilion.[6]

This is not done for the sake of cleanliness; it is a ritual act similar to
many others, such as that performed by the Vallabhacharis of Gujerat
when they immerse the statue of Krishna, dress it and bathe it in milk.
Some people have sought to belittle the profound religious sentiment
that underlies all these rituals, construing them as a way of expressing
'gratitude to the womb'. It has been said, for instance, that
throughout their history the Indians have relied on the cow for their
milk and for help with farm work and cartage—and in this respect
they are, of course, by no means alone—but they also depend on the
cow for fuel since they use dried dung as a source of heat. Has Gandhi
himself not emphasised that 'this gentle animal is a mother to millions
of Indians'? This aspect of the cow as a source of plenty has been symbolised in Hindu mythology by the 'cow of abundance' (*Kâmadhenu*),
who grants to her owner the satisfaction of all his needs. Because he
had taken possession of this talismanic animal by brute force, the King
Kârtavîrya was cut to pieces by the hatchet of Parasu-Râma, one of
the incarnations (*avâtara*) of Vishnu. Surabh, the mythical embodiment of the 'cow of abundance', is one of the 'mothers of beings'
which have filled the universe with their progeny. She gave birth to
the cow, the buffalo and all the other cloven-hoofed animals. When
the God Vishnu enumerated his many incarnations, he took good
care not to forget Surabhî.[7]

This brings us to the sacred texts (*Shruti*), in which, as in all other
aspects of Indian life, the cow occupies a central place, in accordance
with the Indian mentality, so much so that the Vedic
hymns—supposed to be of supernatural origin and to have been
revealed to the ancient sages (*rishi*) by word of mouth—describe the
coming of the day by saying that the day has emerged from its
'byre'—the Night: 'The Dawns (*usha*) have shed their brilliance
upon the Eastern sky. They shine in their glory as the glittering cows
come forth.' There is no reason from a linguistic point of view why

this should be seen as a mere metaphor; it is meant to be a literal account. In another Vedic text, the cow does not symbolise the Day but the Earth: 'The five seasons correspond to the cow of the five names.'[8] According to the commentator Sâyana, the cow of the five names is the Earth, which in spring is called 'the many-blossomed one'; in the summer 'the burnt one'; in the rainy season 'the drenched one'; in the autumn 'the fruitful one'; and in the winter 'the cold one'.

Hardly surprising, therefore, that in the collections of legends (purâna)—the purpose of which was to spread accepted wisdom—similar stories were told. Thus, there is a tale about the demon Kali injuring a cow by kicking it.

To say that it was the cow's usefulness which inspired men to lavish all this respect and even worship on her would thus fall short of the truth. Nor would it do justice to the facts to say that the Indians feel pity for the cow, for the care lavished on her is of an altogether higher order. In fact, the believer is not only enjoined to protect the cow; it is a punishable offence to fail in this duty. These rules are defined in the ancient laws of Manu, which lay down the various penalties meted out to Hindus guilty of having caused the death of a cow:

> He who is guilty of the minor offence of having killed a cow through inadvertence shall shave off all the hair on his head; throughout the whole of one month he shall eat nothing but barley corn boiled in water and shall be confined throughout that time in a piece of cow pasture, covered with the skin of the animal he has killed . . .
>
> He shall follow in the footsteps of the cows all day and every day and, keeping behind them, he shall swallow the dust they kick up with their feet. Having cared for and bowed to them all day, he shall spend the night among and watch over them . . .
>
> Should a cow fall ill or be attacked by brigands and tigers, should a cow fall or sink in a quagmire, he shall do whatever he can to save it . . .[9]

But over and above its sheer usefulness, over and above the glory shed on it by revealed poetry, over and above even the immutable laws handed down through the centuries, there is something in the heart of the Indian which binds, nay rivets, him to the cow and all she stands for—the legend of Krishna.

When the armies of the demons crushed the earth, Bhumî, its personification, sought the protection of Brahmâ, God of Creation, who must not be confused with the Supreme Brahma. Bhumî assumed the form of a cow and, moaning, approached Brahmâ. In this guise, she could be certain of his protection, nor was she disappointed, for Brahmâ brought her case to the notice of the God Vishnu, who decided to manifest part of his being, using his miraculous powers, in the child to whom Devakî, wife of Vasudeva, was about to give birth.

Vasudeva was aware that the perfidious Kamsa, a confederate of the demons, was only looking for a chance to bring about their child's death. Vasudeva, therefore, took the infant, as soon as he was born, to Nanda and Yasodâ, who were to be his foster parents and who were subsequently accepted by the world as his real parents. Nanda was a cowman in charge of a herd grazing on a range (go) bordering the forest of Vrindâvana. The village consisted entirely of cowsheds (gokula) and was inhabited by cowherds (gopa) and herdswomen (gopî).

From his childhood, Krishna displayed tremendous powers, which gradually revealed his supernatural character. Any demons, be they male or female, who dared approach the range either in human guise or as monsters were to rue their temerity for the child had no trouble at all in destroying them by either natural or magic means. As Krishna grew older, the gopî gradually abandoned the cult of the powerful god Indra, attracted by the youngster with his bluish-black hair, who would call them to him playing spell-binding tunes on his flute—tunes which fascinated the gopî so much that they would abandon their cows and their pails in the midst of milking to join him then and there.

Indra thereupon declared that matters could not be left thus and unleashed a cloudburst on the range which threatened to destroy all. Seeing this, Krishna raised the mountain Govardhana from its base to provide shelter for Vasudeva, his staff and all the animals, holding up the mountain with his hand until the storm was over. This feat convinced the people of Krishna's divinity and they henceforth called him 'the Indra of the cows'. Surabhî (the cow of abundance) came down from the 'world of cows' (goloka)—also the heaven of the gods—and said to him: 'Take the place of Indra for us, oh Master of the world! Ensure the happiness of the cows, of the Brahmins, the gods and all well-meaning people.' Indra himself came to make his apologies and crowned Krishna 'King of the Cows'.

From then on, Krishna's bonds with the *gopî* were to become increasingly close. For a time, however, he disappeared, though merely to ensure that his absence would make their hearts grow fonder. Then he danced with the *gopî* in what was to culminate in a Bacchanalian scene, with Krishna being all to each of the herdswomen in turn.

> And as they stamped the ground with their feet, moved their eyebrows graciously and swayed their bodies this way and that, causing their veils to float off their breasts and the locks over their ears to slip down on their cheeks, sweat dampened their faces and their hair and belts came undone. And the wives of Krishna shone as they sang his praises, as a flash of lightning brightens the edge of a cloud.[10]

However, according to the authorities it would be quite wrong to take this account—which as rendered by Jayadeva[11] becomes frankly erotic—at all literally. These are figurative allusions to mystical love, its 'nights' and consolations, with the *gopî* representing souls. The sacred texts themselves tell us that Vishnu's 'descents' must by no means be seen as incarnations: they are symbolic and legendary manifestations of him in the strictly etymological sense of 'legendary', i.e. they were *meant to be read*.

In assuming human shape down here upon earth, Krishna, the Supreme Witness who is manifested in the *gopî*, in their husbands and all living things, is merely enacting a scene. It is out of goodwill for the living world that he takes on human shape and indulges in such games, and he does so in order that people may become attached to him when told of these stories.[12]

To this day the worshippers of Vishnu make pilgrimages to Vrindâvana to commemorate the events described in the legend, which they believe to have been enacted in a figurative and symbolic manner in the heaven of Krishna. In that heaven, all the companions of his earthly life share his level of existence and must hence be divine.

We are, in effect, taught by the holy doctrine (*siddhânta*) that these beings are all 'divided manifestations' of Krishna, i.e. that 'each of them is, in the last resort, Krishna himself personified in a separate body'.[13] Therefore, whenever a worshipper of Vishnu comes face to face with a cow, he feels he is in the presence of the Preserver of the Universe.

The legend of Krishna has given us a picture of the deification of the cow. We can thus see that Gandhi, for all his exaggerated romanticism *à la Tolstoy*, in no way overestimated the place of the cow in the Hindu faith. On the contrary, by adopting a sentimental viewpoint, he failed to do justice to the metaphysical quality of the traditional Hindu outlook, which, while certainly respectful of all forms of life, was more specific in regard to the cow, as we can see from this description given us by L. M. Gauthier: 'To the sages, Surabhî is one of the twelve forms of the Supreme Spirit.'[14]

*   *   *

In many regions of Africa and Asia zebu, or hump-backed cattle, are bred. The origins of this animal remain shrouded in mystery. A figurine of a zebu, some 6,500 years old, has been found in Mesopotamia. The animal spread into China and Africa primarily from India, while into Madagascar it was probably introduced from Indonesia. More recently, the zebu has been imported into tropical America, notably the West Indies.

Farmers cross the species with common cattle. Hybridisation of the Madagascar zebu, the South African zebu and cattle from the Limousin region of France has resulted in the emergence of a breed known as 'Renitelo', with a smaller hump.

Another member of the *Bovidae* family, of great economic importance over vast areas of the world, is the Indian or water buffalo, remarkable for its long curved horns which can be anything up to 1.9 metres long. The animal, which originates from South-East Asia, has virtually disappeared in the wild state. As the name 'water buffalo' indicates, it thrives on marshy land and in rice paddies. In China, India and Indochina it is so widely used as a draught animal that it might be called 'the tractor of Asia'. Rice production largely depends on buffalo breeding, and there can, therefore, be little doubt that the loss of a buffalo may well condemn an entire Asian family to starvation. It is in fact thought that some of the great famines which have ravaged Asia were caused by the massive spread of disease (epizootics) among buffaloes. The buffalo's usefulness as a farm animal is enhanced by the fact that its milk has twice the fat content of cow's milk.

The domestication of the water buffalo is of long standing. From India, the animal was introduced into Egypt, the Balkans and Hungary; and it even reached as far west as Italy. Herds of buffalo can be seen, for instance, in the Danube delta, in Rumania. The famous Balkan yoghurt is made from buffalo milk. There have been several attempts to introduce the buffalo into France. The first of these was made in the twelfth century by the monks of Clairvaux Abbey, and another was inspired by Napoleon I. All these efforts failed, however. On the other hand, the buffalo has been successfully introduced into Australia and Brazil. Several other species of the *Bovidae* family have been domesticated in Asia. In Assam and Burma, the Gayal is bred—an animal which appears to be descended from the Gaur, the big Asian wild bull. In Indonesia, the Banteng—an animal of less heavy build—can be found both in the domesticated and the wild state.

Finally, Tibet and Central Asia in general are the home of an attractive animal, the yak, which has become very rare in the wild state, having been domesticated for centuries. The yak is protected by its shaggy coat from the rigours of the Himalayan and Mongolian climate and can thus live at altitudes of up to 6,000 metres. The yak is of immense economic importance to the peoples of this region, both as a beast of burden and a source of milk and meat; in addition, the Tibetans put yak butter into their tea. It is remarkable that the Incas, with their long-haired llamas, should long, long ago have invented a similar system of animal husbandry. This similarity shows that, given the same set of circumstances, even peoples separated by vast distances are apt to arrive at similar solutions to their problems.

[1] The reader will see in the course of this account that a good many species seem to have been first domesticated in the Middle East. There can be no doubt that this region gave birth to several ancient civilisations. Moreover, its dry soil helps to preserve fossils.

[2] According to recent research, in Mesopotamia and Thessaly the domestication of cattle began even earlier; however, this claim requires further confirmation.

[3] In Nepal, the shepherds twist the horns of their rams together, thus turning the animals into 'unicorns'.

[4] A procession of the fatted ox was held in Paris annually until 1920.

[5] *Young India*, 1921.

[6] *Life* magazine, 7 February 1955.

[7] *Bhagavad-gîtâ*, X, 28.

[8] *Taittirîya-samhitâ*, IV, 11.

[9] *Mânava-dharma-sâstra*, XI, 108.

[10] *Bhâgavata-purâna*, X, 33.

[11] Ibid.

[12] In the Gîtâ-Govinda.

[13] P. Johanns, *La pensée religieuse de l'Inde*, Namur 1952 (Facultés universitaires).

[14] *Bhâgavata-purâna*, Grandeur, III, 35.

CHAPTER FIVE

The Other Ruminants and the Pig

TOGETHER WITH the dog and the sheep, the goat was probably among the first animals to be domesticated. It is descended from the wild goat, or *bouquetin*. The species *Capra hircus*, to which the Alpine ibex belongs, is represented by numerous breeds throughout Europe and Western Asia as far east as Pakistan and it is from the Middle Eastern breeds that the domestic goat appears to be descended.

It seems, in fact to have been first domesticated in the mountains of northern Mesopotamia, i.e. the region now known as Kurdistan. It is believed that this process of domestication took place some time between the years 8050 and 7900 B.C., which means that this is the second oldest process of domestication extant after that of the sheep. Proof of this was obtained when a quantity of goat bones found at Asiab was reliably dated.

In a number of European countries goats—other than the true wild goat—can be found which are either wild or at least have reverted to the wild state. They have retained the agility of their ancestors and skip about freely among the rocks. Such goats are known to exist on the Greek islands, on the Italian island of Monte Cristo (made famous by Alexandre Dumas), in Wales, Ireland, Scotland and other countries. Those in Crete—and perhaps also those in Bulgaria—may be regarded as true wild goats. In Corsica and in the Alps, flocks of goats can, moreover, be seen roaming at liberty during the spring and summer.

Useful though it may be for its milk, skin and hair, the 'poor man's cow' does a great deal of damage. It does much harm to vegetation owing to its liking for shoots, an addiction which interferes with the renewal of plant life. Goats nibble the grass down to the roots, and trample and kill it altogether near the watering places they frequent on their long treks.

The goat has been accused, no doubt with some exaggeration, of having devastated the forests of the Mediterranean Basin. From the beginning of the seventeenth century onward measures were taken to control the goat, which was not allowed into the forests where trees, earmarked for shipbuilding, were grown.

In Africa, the goat does not merely nibble at trees, it climbs them nimbly, despite the fact that hooves are by no means the best equipment for this sort of exercise. In Morocco, the goats climb to the very top of the *arganier* trees. They eat the pulp of the fruit but not the stones, which the local people collect carefully and press to produce cooking oil.

The island of St. Helena, in the South Atlantic, was covered with thick forest until 1513, in which year goats were introduced there. By 1588, they had increased in number to several thousand. By 1745 only a handful of tiny patches of forest were left, and when Napoleon first glimpsed the island from his ship it had been totally denuded by the goats.

Goats, both male and female, feature in the mythology of many cultures. The 'Goat of Mendes' was worshipped in Egypt. This male goat personified four gods—Ra, Osiris, Geb and Shu. However, there does not appear to be a very clear distinction between this creature and the 'Ram of Mendes'. The he-goat generally stands for lust and passion. Witches used to be depicted riding a Billy goat on their way to their sabbaths, gatherings presided over by Satan in the guise of that animal. The beard and smell of the he-goat have undoubtedly inspired these myths. The Satyrs were creatures half man half goat. As for the scapegoat, this is a theme which occurs throughout the world, to as far away as Japan. In the folk tales of black Africa, the he-goat is a cunning and deceitful creature, brimming over with lust, and is accused by the Africans of all sorts of sexual perversions.

The theme of the male goat is not without its tragic aspects: in fact, the very word *tragedy* literally means 'song of the he-goat'. Originally it denoted the ritual chanting which accompanied the sacrifice of a male goat to Dionysos. The animal served both this god and Pan as a mount, and both were depicted dressed in a goat's skin. The male goat, being the symbol of sexual ardour, was one of the animals sacred to Aphrodite. In Ireland, the *goborchind*, (i.e. goat's heads) are inferior beings of repulsive appearance. However, in India, the goat's position in mythology is more flattering: it is the symbol of procreative fire, the source of life.

In India, too, a she-goat—believed to be red, white and black—the colours which symbolise creation—is the Mother of the World (or Prakriti). In China and Tibet, the she-goat is associated with lightning, and in Greece, too, it used to symbolise this natural phenomenon. In the Bible, the cloth of the tabernacle was said to be made of goat's hair, in memory of the flashes of lightning which accompanied the appearance of God on Mount Sinai. Finally, we must not forget to mention the little goat which was the pet of Esmeralda, the heroine of Victor Hugo's *Hunchback of Notre Dame*.

* * *

If the wild goat was the ancestor of the domestic goat, that of the sheep was the moufflon. The various breeds of sheep are in fact descended from several European and Asian species of the moufflon.

The short-tailed, dark-horned breeds would seem to be derived from the Corsican moufflon, which has survived to this day on that island as well as in Sardinia and Cyprus. This splendid beast, which has a russet, black or white fleece and curved horns, has been introduced into a number of regions of Europe, such as, for instance, the Cevennes mountains of France.

The breeds which sport a longer tail and light-coloured horns are believed to be descended from another moufflon—the *Argali* of Central Asia, which has a brown fleece and can have remarkably big horns. A third species, the *Urial*, which comes from the same region, is probably the ancestor of several Asian breeds.

The sheep was without a doubt the first animal to be domesticated. The process began in Kurdistan in the ninth millennium B.C.—a hypothesis borne out by the finds made at the archaeological sites of Zevi Shemi and Shamidar. Other remains of domesticated sheep have been found at Jarmo, in Mesopotamia, and at Argissa, in Thessaly, both dating from approximately 7000 B.C. It is believed that the domestication of the sheep proceeded independently in the Orient and the Balkans. Different breeds developed at a very early stage—a fact proved by the discovery of two distinct types of sheep at lake settlement sites in the Alps.

The sheep accomplished vast migrations across the world along with its pastoral owners, with the result that the geographical distribution of the various breeds changed continually. The best known is the Merino, with a thick, woolly fleece. It is believed to originate from Africa and was introduced into Spain by the Arabs towards the end of the eleventh century. The Merino became the object of armed conflict between the Moors and the Spaniards since the former controlled the southern regions of Spain and thus the richer pastures. The name Merino comes from *merinas*, the name given to the Spanish officials whose duty it was to supervise the allocation of pasture rights.

At a later stage, British wool came on to the market and was sold in competition with the wool of the Merino. We are now speaking of the sixteenth century, the time of the 'wool revolution'. Crop cultivation in the two countries, Spain and Britain, gave way to sheep breeding and it was not very long before most of the farming land carried sheep. This invasion was not to everybody's liking and pamphlets began to appear which said, for example: 'Sheep have stripped our meadows and our land, our corn and our forests, whole cities and villages.' Another said: 'God gave the earth to man to dwell on, not not to sheep and game.'[1] On the other hand, sheep breeding enabled the British to establish the world's biggest textile industry.

In France, it was Daubenton, a collaborator of Buffon, who first introduced the Merino on his farm at Montbard in the Cote-d'Or Department. The breed was later improved at the national sheep stud at Rambouillet, and from there it has spread to all parts of the world.

Another breed which has long been popular is the Karakul, from

Central Asia. Since before the year 1000 B.C. the peoples of this region are known to have traded the fleece of this sheep, better known by the name Astrakhan, in neighbouring countries. The breed was introduced into France in 1943. Unfortunately, it is only the skin of still-born or very young lambs which have any value. The pelt is then black and curly, while that of the adult sheep is grey and smooth. The producers therefore deliberately cause the ewes to abort in order to obtain these skins.

Just as there are goats which have reverted to the wild state, so there are sheep on some of the islands off the coast of Scotland and England, notably on the island of Soay, in the Inner Hebrides, which have done likewise.

The lamb and the ram have played a prominent part in religion and mythology. The former has always been a symbol of gentleness, purity and innocence. In Christianity it plays an important role as the symbol of the Saviour. There is a link between the biblical lamb and the Vedic God of Fire, Agni, who is carried on the back of a ram. In the Bible, the lamb plays the part, above all, of sacrificial victim; it is featured in the same role in Islam, while in the religion of ancient Greece the God Dionysos is pictured as sacrificing a lamb to appease Cerberus.

In ancient Egypt, the ram symbolised power and was the emblem of the God of Air and Fruitfulness, Amon or Ammon. At Herakleopolis the Egyptians worshipped the Ram God Harsaphes, and the 'Ram of Mendes', which was believed to shelter the souls of Osiris and Râ, was also held in high regard by the Egyptians. Like the bull Apis, Harsaphes was a god in his own right and not merely the symbol of a god. The Egyptians mummified numerous rams.

In India, the Goddess Kuvera rode on a ram, and in China rams played a part in ordeals. The ram symbolised fruitfulness not only in Egypt but also in Gaul, and the same theme is current among the Dogon people of Mali. The latter have pictured a ram on the wall of a sanctuary, side by side with a maize cob; its tail was depicted as ending in a snake's head. As for the Dorians, they worshipped Apollo in the shape of a ram. In one of the temples of Boeotia, Hermes Krio-phoros—'the carrier of the ram'—was venerated in recognition of the fact that he had wiped out a plague raging among animals by carrying a ram on his shoulders. This legend is reflected in numerous

Christian works of art which feature a shepherd carrying a lamb on his shoulders.

       *   *   *

Camels, both of the single and of the twin-humped varieties, are part and parcel of the life of the world's arid regions, steppe and desert alike. Asia is the home of the Bactrian, or twin-humped camel. The animal has become very rare in the wild state, though some wild Bactrian camels have survived in Central Asia. Some four to five hundred are in fact known to exist in south-west Mongolia, and others in north-west China. These camels have been the subject of much controversy: some zoologists at one time believed the animals to be descended from domesticated animals which had reverted to the wild state. However, it is now generally accepted that these are in fact genuinely wild animals.

It was probably in Bactria, the present Afghanistan, that this species was first domesticated in the third millennium B.C. The Bactrian camel is pictured on the bas-reliefs of Persepolis. At the time of Darius, caravans of 5,000 camels made their way down from the mountains to that city each year. In 480 B.C., the camels of Xerxes' army were attacked by lions (believe it or not!) in the Mount Athos area. The Bactrian camel is still used throughout Central Asia (the Pamir region, Mongolia, etc.) for riding, and it can be found as far west as the Crimea. In times gone by it was used further west still and hence, much to the surprise of the archaeologists concerned, when the amphitheatre of the Roman city of Lutetia (the present Paris) was excavated in 1870, the skeletons of camels were discovered. In fact, the Goths had introduced the camel into Western Europe by way of the Danube Valley, and it is to a camel that Queen Brunhilda was said to have been tied before being lashed to a horse and torn limb from limb.

The dromedary has only one hump, and no longer exists in the wild state. The Arabs first domesticated it in South-West Asia. Later, and independently, it was domesticated in the northern Sahara. The dromedary is mentioned in the Bible, and was depicted by Assyrian artists.

In our own day, the 'ship of the desert'—the *mehari* of the Arabs—is used as a beast of burden throughout North and North-East Africa and as far south as Kenya, as well as in Western Asia as far as Afghanistan. In the areas where the two species are found side by side, they interbreed.

The dromedary was introduced into the Cadiz region of Spain, where it is still used for carrying water and wood. It has also been introduced into Australia and the United States; in the latter country a small number of camels reverted to the wild state and for a time lived in the Arizona Desert before becoming extinct. Perhaps we should add that both species of camel provide meat, milk and wool.

Camels are also found in the Andean Cordillera, but the species in question has no humps. We are talking, of course, of the llama, of which four varieties exist, regarded as four breeds of one and the same species: the vicuna, the guanaco, the llama proper and the alpaca. The first of these exists to all intents in the wild state only and is now nearly extinct. The second, also wild, appears to have been the ancestor of the last two, which are domesticated. The guanaco was domesticated by the Indians, above all the Incas, before Columbus' discovery of America. The llama is used as a pack animal: because it is so sure-footed it can negotiate even the steepest trails in the Andes. However, it will on no account carry a rider. The heavy-fleeced alpaca, on the other hand, is bred for its wool, and it was from alpaca hair that the Incas used to weave their cloth.

The llama is a gentle and even-tempered animal; its only way of defending itself is to spit in the face of anyone who annoys or teases it.

*   *   *

The *Cervidae* family includes only one important domesticated species, the reindeer. The fallow deer which is purely an ornamental animal lives in semi-liberty in the parks of Europe, the continent of its origin. Buck-skin, used, among other things, for shoe making, comes for the most part from America.

The reindeer is *the* domestic animal of the Far North of Europe. Its most remarkable characteristic is that not only the male but the female, too, has antlers. The animals were found in large numbers in Western Europe towards the end of the Quaternary, for which reason the latter is sometimes called the Reindeer Age.

Subsequently, the reindeer withdrew to more northern latitudes. We know very little about the domestication of the reindeer; it is said to have been accomplished comparatively recently—towards the end of the ninth century. However, as early as prehistoric times the reindeer's bones and antlers were used by man, and a great many rock paintings exist of the animal. Thanks to the work of Prof. A. Leroi-Gourhan, we are able to formulate certain hypotheses regarding the process of the reindeer's domestication. We know that reindeer migrate annually in vast herds. The migrations of the caribou, the American reindeer, are a byword. In certain regions of Scandinavia and Eastern Siberia, the herds follow the course of enclosed valleys since no other route is available to them to reach the lower regions, where they stay in the winter, from the high pastures where they spend the summer. This process is put to good use by man, who simply follows the herds without seeking to influence their choice of route. In other words, this is a case of man adapting himself to the animal rather than the other way round.

In other regions, the reindeer's domestication has been taken a step further: the older males are castrated, which does away with competition for the females. In this way, larger herds can be formed, with the younger males alone ensuring the propagation of the species.

In the Arctic zone, the reindeer is put to many uses by the population. It serves as a draught animal, it provides milk, meat, leather, fur and even the antlers are used as fish hooks. Lapp civilisation largely depends on the reindeer, just as that of the Tibetans is based on the yak and as that of the Incas relied on the llama. Since 1910, reindeer have been imported into a number of islands in the Antarctic.

*   *   *

With the pig, we are in more familiar territory. The pig has one point in common with the reindeer: it, too, has its origins in the forest. It should be borne in mind, incidentally, that the reindeer spends part of each year in the forest. However, the majority of domesticated hoofed animals come from the steppes and prairies.

The pig is descended from the wild boar, or to be more exact, from several varieties of that animal. The European boar (*Sus scrofa*) is undoubtedly one of the ancestors of the domesticated pig, and so most certainly is a smaller animal—the Indian or Malay pig (*Sus vittatus*). It is from this species that the small Asian pig is descended, which—we do not know how—spread at a very early stage to Europe, for remains of this species have been found side by side with those of *Sus scrofa* at the sites of prehistoric lake settlements.

We are in a position to make some intelligent guesses as to the way the boar was domesticated, at least in Europe north of the Alps. In that region, the pig was undoubtedly the second-earliest animal to be domesticated, after the dog. In the first place, wild pigs—so the theory goes—must have approached man on their own initiative, attracted by domestic refuse. Remains of domesticated pigs have been found at the Greek site of Argissa already mentioned (7000 B.C.), and remains found in Turkey are said to date from the same period. We know, moreover, that boars are easy to tame, and it is said that they were at times also used in warfare.

At all events, pig breeding was the most important branch of animal husbandry in the neolithic age and spread very rapidly across the whole of the Old World. The Egyptians, Greeks and Romans all allowed their pigs to live in a state of semi-liberty in the forests, where they were left to fend for themselves by rooting in the ground. The Romans were familiar with the Asian breed—a fact which emerges from the author Columella's description of a pig with short legs and a flat snout. The breed can still be found in the Far East; it is remarkable for the size of the body and the shortness of the legs. In Europe, it was only in the eighteenth century that pig breeding and selection were seriously attempted.

It goes without saying that the pig plays an important part in mythology. It was sacrificed to the Goddess Demeter, and Homer tells us that the comrades of Ulysses were changed into piglets by the sorceress Circe. In the Middle Ages, pigs were allowed to wander freely about the streets of Paris, together with hens, geese and ducks, and acted as scavengers. Unfortunately, this freedom accorded to the pig led to accidents: pigs would occasionally kill children, and were then tried for murder. We shall deal with this practice later on.

In 1131, pigs caused the horse of a son of King Louis VI to fall. The Prince was killed and pigs were thereafter banished from the streets of the capital. In 1368, however, the monks of the Order of St. Anthony were authorised to allow their pigs to wander freely about Paris, on one condition: they had to have the Greek letter 'Tau'—the emblem of St. Anthony—branded on one shoulder. The Friars of St. Anthony used to beg for alms holding their porkers on a lead.

The pig was accused of being the incarnation of the devil. In the New Testament, devils say to Christ: 'Send us into the swine, that we may enter into them.' The pig played an important part in Polynesia and above all in New Guinea, where it is known to have been domesticated in 3000 B.C. The pig, incidentally, to this day serves the people of that island as the sole source of meat. Papuan women breast-feed their piglets, which are treated as members of the tribe. Conversely, a sow suckling two human infants is depicted on a column in Metz Cathedral. In Congolese folklore, Tata Gulube—'fat father pig'—is said to have fought and killed a panther.

In tropical America, the Peccary pig is sometimes kept by farmers in a state of semi-freedom, which shows how readily pigs allow themselves to be domesticated.

[1] According to R. Lewinsohn, *Histoire des Animaux*, Plon, 1953.

CHAPTER SIX

From the Horse to the Elephant

ALL THAT there is to be said about man's noblest conquest has been said, and yet the earliest history of the horse is far from clear; in fact, it is a distinctly complicated jigsaw puzzle. The horse as we know it today is the result of a long process of evolution which the palaeontologists have managed to trace as far back as the Eocene, i.e. the beginning of the Tertiary era.

Its earliest ancestor was an animal no bigger than a fox. This was the *Hyracotherium*, whose home was in Europe, while a similar animal, the *Eohippus*, lived in America. These venerable forefathers of the horse already had an elongated muzzle, but their feet still had four toes. Subsequently, in the course of the evolution of the horse family, the number of toes gradually diminished. By the end of the Oligocene, the *Miohippus* had attained the size of our present-day sheep. It was followed by the *Protohippus* and the *Pliohippus*. These various ancestors of the horse lived in America, and it was in that continent that the horse first appeared during the Upper Pliocene.

Moreover, it fairly soon became extinct in America—this, at any rate, is the classic theory, which may, however, have to be revised. We shall return to this subject later. But before the horse died out in America, it first spread to the Old World.

Prehistoric man was quite familiar with the wild horse, which at that time inhabited Eurasia. He hunted these animals and made paintings of them on the walls of his caves. J. Blanchard, an expert on the prehistoric era, believes he can identify in these paintings distinct breeds—the bearded horse, the Pyrenean horse, the short-tailed horse, etc.

It is among these breeds that we must look for the ancestors of our modern domestic horse. Horses which are more or less wild still exist to this day, though the majority are animals which have merely reverted to the wild state. The famous white horse of the Camargue, which, mane flying in the wind, races across the salt flats, is one such breed. Others are the Exmoor pony of England, the Mustang of the American Far West and the Polish *Konik*. Breeds of horses which have gone wild can also be found in a number of other countries including Germany, Spain, Sweden and Iceland.

Among French breeds, in addition to the Camargue horse, we ought to mention the Landes breed (well known for its fierce kick and very difficult to catch), the Ariege horse and, above all, the Pottok horse of the Basque country.[1] The Pottok is a small horse with either an all-black or a piebald coat, and the breed is certainly very ancient. The Pottok's blood has special characteristics which make it useful for human grafts. For all these reasons, a national society has been established for the protection of the Pottok breed.

However, side by side with these horses which have reverted to a state of relative freedom, genuinely wild horses—the *Tarpans*—have existed in Europe until recently. These animals survived in the Alps, in Germany and in Denmark until the Middle Ages; in fact, in Lithuania and Prussia they maintained themselves until the sixteenth century. They stood some 12 hands tall and had light grey coats, with light stripes on the forelegs, while their manes were dark and *en brosse*.

There were two breeds of the *Tarpan*—the forest *Tarpan* (*Equus caballus silvaticus*), which lived in Poland and was the first to become extinct, and the steppe *Tarpan* (*Equus caballus gmelini*), which did not die out until about 1880 and whose home was in Southern Russia.

Just like the Aurochs, the *Tarpan* cannot be regarded as a truly 'lost' animal, for by crossing various breeds which have reverted to the wild state it has been possible to 'reconstruct' the *Tarpan* more or less accurately.

In the late 1870s, an officer in the Russian cavalry, Przewalski,[2] discovered in the steppes of Central Asia a hitherto unknown member of the horse family—unknown, that is, among extant horse breeds at least, since it closely resembled various prehistoric breeds. This animal stands thirteen hands tall, has a very large head with short ears, a yellowish-brown coat and has its mane *en brosse*, while its body is remarkable for its stoutness. The breed has since been known as *Przewalski's horse*; it closely resembles the horses depicted on rock paintings, bones of which have been discovered by palaeontologists.

*   *   *

The horse was first domesticated somewhere in Eurasia, but it is hard to say exactly where. In fact, the process may have occurred in several places at more or less the same time. The Caucasians and the Ukrainians appear to have succeeded in domesticating the horse during the fourth and third millennia B.C. According to a recently published theory, in the Ukraine this process occurred some time between 4300 and 3700 B.C. From there, the art of domesticating the horse is said to have spread westward and to have reached Germany some time after 3600 and eventually also the British Isles and Africa. Rock paintings featuring horses either carrying riders or pulling chariots have been found in the Tassili mountains in the Sahara. However, at roughly the same time the Mongols also seem to have tamed the horse. At all events, one thing is certain: it was somewhere in the steppes of Eurasia, between Hungary and Manchuria, that the horse was first conquered by man.

Thanks to several pieces of archaeological evidence, we are able to trace the various stages of this conquest. The first paintings of the horse to be made in Mesopotamia date from the beginning of the third millennium: the Sumerians at first used wild asses to pull their carts; later they replaced the ass with the horse. A curb chain found near Odessa, which dates from the end of the first millennium, proves that by that time the horse had been trained. Also, a two-wheel cart dating from the same time has been found near Dnepropetrovsk.

In the Bible, the horse is not mentioned as being among the 'wealth' of Job, but the book of Samuel speaks of a Philistine cavalry

force of 6,000 men. We are also told that it was on horseback that the
Egyptians pursued the Jews across the desert. It is a fact that the horse
appeared in Nubia and Egypt at a comparatively early stage: herds of
horses are known to have been kept in the Nile Delta. The Egyptians
called the horse 'the beautiful one' while the Babylonians described
it, perhaps rather paradoxically, as 'animal of the mountains'. The
horse played a very important part among the Persians. According to
Herodotus, Darius was chosen from several pretenders to be King
because his horse had been the first to neigh to greet the rising sun.

The horse acquired considerable importance in Greece, where it
was regarded, above all, as the symbol of perfect movement and
hence of musical rhythm. The cult of the wild horse was one of the
oldest rites of Greek religion. By striking the ground with his trident,
Poseidon made the horse Arion emerge from the earth. The horses of
Greek mythology symbolised the motion of the waves. They first
pulled Poseidon's chariot and then took off into the air, beating their
wings. For these were indeed winged horses, and the most famous of
them was Pegasus. Most of the heroes of Greek mythology and
history had their favourite mounts: Bucephalus was Alexander the
Great's charger, while Balios and Xanthos were given to Achilles by
his father. At the spot where Alexander's horse died the city of Buce-
phala was founded. The Pegasus theme was taken up again in the
Middle Ages with the Hippogryph.

In the steppes of Central Asia—the favourite stamping ground of
the horse—people were apt to credit the animal with supernatural
powers: they used to believe, for instance, in the horse of the chthonic
world[3] which guided the souls of the dead. There was also the legend
of the magic horse Chal-Kuyruk, the hero of the Kirghiz epic of Er-
Tostük. This horse asked its master to rip great chunks of flesh out of
its body by means of his whip as a sort of initiation ceremony which
would restore the animal's lost powers. The horse played a part in
numerous shamanic[4] rites of Central Asia. When a horseman died, his
mount would be buried with him to help him on his last journey. The
members of the Beltir tribe sacrificed the horse to its dead master—a
practice which is one of the characteristic features of primitive Asian
cultures.

This ritual spread as far as the Mediterranean; thus, Achilles
sacrificed a number of mares in honour of his friend Patroclus. A.
Gheerbrant has drawn attention to the fact that there is a distinct

resemblance between the stick shaped to resemble a horse's neck and head (or horse-stick) on which the Shamans of Central Asia claimed to ride into the other world, and the broomstick of the European witches.

According to Indian legend the tenth and last *avâtar*[5] of Vishnu is the horse Kalki which, with a single blow of its hoof, will one day reduce the world to dust. In many cultures the horse symbolised fruitfulness. The Gauls and the Celts of Ireland worshipped the goddess Epona, whose name meant 'the Great Mare'. She was depicted as sitting on a horse flanked by a mare and her colt. The mare-goddess Rhianon was Epona's counterpart in Wales.

In Northern Ireland a strange enthronement ritual was celebrated around 1185: a white mare was killed and her flesh boiled in water. The future sovereign was first immersed in this water and then ate the animal's flesh. The sacrifice of the horse (or *Asvamedha*) practised in India was a somewhat similar ceremony. In fact, this resemblance is one of many indications of the oneness of the Indo-European world. In Rome, a horse was sacrificed each year on 15 October, after the end of the harvest. Its head would be adorned with corn as a sign of gratitude for the success of the harvest, and the animal's tail clipped. In this ritual, the horse personified the grain crop. In France, it was always the youngest horse which was honoured at the harvest festival, for it was believed that the success of the next sowing depended on that animal.

Sometimes the horse was also venerated as a water godhead. The fishermen of the Volga region used to drown a horse at the time of the thaw as an offering to the 'Grandfather of the Waters'. The ancient Greeks seemed to follow a similar practice. In Europe as in Asia the horse was believed to be able to make a spring burst forth by stamping the ground with its hoof. This is how Pegasus created the Hippocrene fountain, whose waters served as a source of poetic inspiration, and it was another magic horse, Morvac'h, in the Breton legend of the town of Ys, which, by leaping over the waves, enabled Malgven and Grallon to rejoin the Breton fleet. It was also on Morvac'h that Grallon managed to escape the raging sea when it engulfed the town of Ys. When the Saxons invaded England, they scratched the silhouettes of horses into the chalky slopes of Wessex, for their emblem was the horse. In Cambodian folklore, a horse races through the night, pulling behind it around the world a cart laden

MAA

with precious stones and with the Moon seated in it. In all these stories, the horse symbolises speed.

In demonology, three types of horses must be distinguished. There is the spirited white charger which in the Vendée region of France causes travellers to lose their way. Another evil horse—this one in the Jura—also attacks travellers—but this animal only has three legs. The third is a black horse which is the devil's favourite mount. It was on such a horse that Faust and Mephistopheles rode to the witches' sabbath.

The white horse is a symbol of Venus and of various concepts associated with the planet of that name, such as love, light and liberation. The sacred horses of the peoples which once inhabited Germany, Ireland and India were all white.

In ancient China, the initiates of secret societies were known as 'horse traders', and to arrange a secret meeting was called to 'give the horses their head'.

In Hebrew, the word for horse is rendered by means of three letters—written of course in the Oriental manner from right to left: Lamed—Vau—Shin. The first, Lamed, means 'rising movement'; Shin stands for fire and light, and Vau is the link which unites Lamed and Shin. In other words, the word for horse, in writing, symbolises here an ascent towards the light.

Since the days of classical antiquity, the horse has been the symbol of death. For Artemidorus, to dream of a horse was to have a premonition of death. The Harpies, demons of death, sometimes assumed the appearance of mares. Ronsard, in his hymns, speaks of an evil black horse:

> I saw beside me, mounted on a great black steed

> A man made but of bone. On seeing him As he offered me his hand to help me mount behind

> A trembling fear ran through my bones.

However, phantom horses are not always black; they can also be pale, but never white. Their very palour is a reminder of death. Every whit as evil as the black horse, these pale chargers are messengers of impending death, especially in French and German folklore. In the Book of Apocalypse (VI, 8), St. John recounts: 'And I saw a horse of pale colour. He who rode on it was called Death, and Hell followed him.' In Breton mythology, there were horses which caused travellers to lose their way in the marshes. *Mahrt*, a German mare-devil, is said to be at the root of both the French word *cauchemar* and the English *nightmare*. A much more recent myth is the one about the bald charger, blind and without a mane, which the survivors of Hiroshima claim to have seen roaming among the ruins of their city.

* * *

The invention of the harness, in the Middle Ages, was of great importance since it contributed to the disappearance of slavery and, of course, the age of chivalry would certainly never have dawned without the domestication of the horse.

In the last century, horses were used in the coalmines. In his *Germinal*, Emile Zola gave us a moving picture of the old pit pony Bataille welcoming a newcomer, Trompette.

> Soon Trompette was lying on the iron flooring, an inert mass. Still he did not move, but seemed lost in the nightmare of this black and endless cavern, this vast chamber full of noises. As they were setting about untying him, up came Bataille, who had just been unharnessed. He stretched his neck and sniffed at this new pal who had dropped down from the earth . . . Perhaps he found in his new friend the good smell of the open air, the long-forgotten smell of the sun-kissed grass, for all of a sudden he burst into a resounding whinny, a song of joy with a sob of wistfulness running through it. This was his act of welcome, made up of delight in this fragrance of the old, far-off things and sadness that here was one more prisoner who would never go back alive.[6]

The pit ponies were thick-set, muscular creatures, no more than 13 hands high. Their task was to haul trolleys, or 'tubs', along rail tracks. Each tub weighed 250 kg empty and double that when loaded. The ponies were expected to pull a train of anything from ten to twenty of these vehicles over an average distance of some 300 metres. Their task was made easier by a slight downward slope. The good pit ponies shared the hard life of the men, women and children with whom they worked. They were carefully looked after by veterinary surgeons, and this was indeed necessary for the animals were subject to bouts of colic and would occasionally suffer a stroke, not to speak of their many minor injuries. At the end of the day's work, the pony would be led to its underground stable; it was never taken above ground. The story is told of a pit-pony which completed twenty-three years of service . . .

                    *   *   *

Let us return at this point to the problem of the horse's presence in America. It is generally thought that the horse had vanished from that continent well before the arrival of the white man, so that the Indians never saw a horse until the Spanish conquest. It is said that when the *Conquistadores* invaded the New World, mounted on horseback, the Indians were scared at the sight of these 'centaurs', and the surprise caused by the animals is said to have made the conquerors' task easier.

Certain palaeontological and archaeological discoveries, however, compel us to modify this view. In a recent article Simone Waisbard[7] summarised these findings. Earlier, Darwin had found the bones of a prehistoric member of the horse family in Argentina. Later, the carcass of a horse—estimated to be 50,000 years old—which had been buried and preserved in quicksand was excavated near Machu-Picchu (in Peru). Other remains have been examined in Ecuador, Brazil and other South American countries by the famous anthropologist Paul Rivet.

The most remarkable find was that of the bones and pieces of skin of a horse of more recent date, estimated to be only between 8,000 and 9,500 years old. It would therefore seem that horses survived in South America until much later than had been supposed. But were these animals domesticated? This is by no means impossible. In fact, the Swiss explorer Jean-Christian Spahni discovered in the caves of Mazo-Druz, near Lake Titicaca, rock paintings of men on horseback. The animals depicted could only have been horses since the paintings feature the characteristic tail which distinguishes the horse from all other animals. These rock paintings are between 4,000 and 10,000 years old.

There is another piece of evidence to be taken into consideration in this context: According to the Chinese traveller Hue Shan, who is said to have discovered America (by the Pacific route) in the fifth century A.D., the Indians used horses as draught animals to pull carts. The species in question (*Equus andinus*) disappeared before the Spanish conquest. We must assume, however, that the domestication of this animal had not advanced very far, for truly domesticated species do not die out. It is the puma, incidentally, which is said to have been responsible for wiping out the horse from the American continent . . .

*   *   *

In our own time, when people speak of horses what they really have in mind is as often as not racing (and the jackpot). Horse racing, by the way, is by no means a novelty, for the Olympic Games of classical antiquity included races for riders on horseback as well as chariot races, the chariots being pulled by either two or four horses.

During the late Roman Empire, people took a passionate interest in horse racing, which took place in the circuses. The same was true of Byzantium, where racing aroused tremendous passions: one race was followed by riots which led to 40,000 people being killed . . . In France, horse racing was first introduced in the fifth century. The most famous meetings were those at Moorlaz, the ancient capital of the Béarn region. Later, the sport became fashionable in other countries, above all in England, while in France it suffered an eclipse and did not return until the eighteenth century.

The machine age resulted in a marked decline in the number of horses kept: they were gradually displaced from the European countryside by the tractor. In other words, h.p. was preferred to the horse. In recent years, however, the horse has undoubtedly been coming back into its own.

Pony-trekking has become fashionable, and various equestrian events have been included in the Olympic programme. Moreover, riding has also been adopted as a method of physiotherapy to help handicapped children. At the same time, the circus, rodeos and polo are as popular as ever. The latter game was invented in Persia in the sixth century. From there, it spread to India, where it was taken up by the British. Let us briefly recall that polo is a ball game played on grass by two teams of four riders each.

Throughout the length and breadth of France pony clubs, where the horsemen and horsewomen of the future receive their training, are being set up for the benefit of children. As for the ponies themselves, they are—as everyone knows—small horses, frequently of island origin. Incidentally, they are one of the most striking examples of *nanosomia*, or dwarfism, induced by island conditions.

*   *   *

The poor relation of the horse, the donkey—celebrated by the French poet Francis Jammes—comes from North Africa and has survived there in the wild state on the borders of Ethiopia and Somalia. There can be no doubt, however, that these wild asses are not the ancestors of the domestic donkey. The latter is descended from the Nubian ass—which probably no longer exists in pure-bred form—or the Algerian ass, which died out more than 2,000 years ago.

Having been domesticated in the Mediterranean Basin long, long ago, the donkey has throughout retained an important place in that region. In ancient Egypt, it was regarded as a symbol of the gods Râ and Typhon (Set). It was considered an unclean beast and was represented with a knife thrust into its back. According to the religious beliefs of ancient Egypt, the human soul, after death, encountered the awesome red ass. This belief perhaps lives on in the French expression '*méchant comme un âne rouge*' (vicious as a red donkey). Similarly, there may be a connection between the Scarlet Beast of the Apocalypse and the Egyptian red ass. All sorts of healing properties were attributed to the donkey's hair, bones and milk: Cleopatra used to bathe in ass's milk.

The ass also played a role in the cult of Apollo. The Greeks and Romans criticised the Christians for revering the donkey, and the donkey does indeed appear in a favourable light in various New Testament episodes, from the nativity to the flight into Egypt and Christ's entry into Jerusalem to the welcome of a crowd waving palm fronds. The she-ass of the magician Balaam is the only animal credited by the Bible with the power of speech. Quite recently, blasphemous *graffiti* drawings have been discovered near Bethlehem which show Christ in the guise of a donkey. They are believed to be the work of a follower of the 'Messiah' Bar-kokba, who, about A.D. 135, led a Jewish rising against the Romans.

In general, however, the donkey has always been despised by the ancient Egyptians as well as the Jews and the Moslems. There was a time, however, when ass's ears were the attribute of a king. In fact, Apollo caused the King of Phrygia, Midas, to grow ass's ears because the king had taken sides against him in a musical contest between himself and Pan. Only Midas' barber knew of the King's affliction. Unable to keep the secret to himself, he confided it to a hole he dug in the ground. However, the reeds which grew in that spot overheard the dread secret, and every time the wind blew, their rustling would give it away: 'Midas, King Midas has ass's ears.'

During the second century A.D., the Roman author Apuleius wrote his novel *The Golden Ass* in which he tells of the fortunes of a young man-changed-into-animal. In the Middle Ages, a 'Donkey Festival' used to be celebrated at Beauvais. A richly adorned donkey was led into a church, where its braying made a strange accompaniment to the hymns and sacred music. At Sens, religious songs were sung in honour of the animal, which indeed plays an important part in proverbs and folk tales the world over. The story of the ass's skin, which is of oriental origin, became popular in France in the sixteenth century, and Perrault put it into rhyme in 1715. The story is about a princess who, to escape her father, runs away from home disguised in an ass's skin and finally marries a prince.

The donkey also played a part in an amusing practical joke. A picture exhibition in Paris included a canvas entitled 'Sunset over the Adriatic'. The author of this highly successful painting, a certain Boronali, had not yet made his mark in the world of fashion. He was indeed a rather exceptional character: some clever young bloods in Montmartre, including the writer Roland Dorgelès, had in fact tied a brush to the tail of a donkey, and it is by moving that part of its anatomy that the animal produced the much-admired canvas. If the exhibition organisers had had their wits about them, they would have tumbled to the fact that Boronali is an anagram of Aliboron, a donkey which figures in one of La Fontaine's fables.

*   *   *

With the next animal, there is no need for elaborate research into its origins for we are dealing with a creature that has been brought into this world by man: the Mule, a cross between a donkey and a mare. This hybridisation has been practised since time immemorial, for the mule is mentioned both in the Bible and the *Iliad*.

That the ancient Gauls were familiar with the mule is clear from the fact that Epona was regarded as the goddess not only of the horse but of the mule as well. In the fourth century, St. Hilary, Bishop of Poitiers, used a mule to travel from place to place, and in the Middle Ages the mule was indeed the most popular means of transport with the clergy and judiciary alike.

The mule which won the greatest literary fame was without doubt the mount of the good Pope Boniface, immortalised by Alphonse Daudet. This is how Daudet described it:

> He was a fine black mule with red markings, sure of foot and with a shining coat, a large, ample rump and a small, lean head which he carried proudly. He was tricked out with bows, pompoms, silver bells and rosettes, but for all that he was as gentle as an angel, with his ingenuous look and two long ears, always nodding up and down, which gave him a good-natured appearance.

This was the time when there were Popes in residence in Avignon. Boniface lavished care on his mule. But unfortunately for the animal, the Pope one day took on as a servant a scamp by the name of Tistet Védène, who subjected the poor mule to all kinds of torments, even forcing it to climb to the the top of a steeple . . .

Soon after this episode, Tistet left for Naples, where he remained for seven years. The mule, however, did not forget its persecutor. When Tistet returned to Avignon, he persuaded the Pope to appoint him his mustard maker, a most important post. The mule attended the ceremony of Tistet's assumption of office, and when he was within reach of the rogue let go with his hooves for all he was worth, so that all that was left of Tistet was a cloud of dust . . .

It is by no means always easy to induce a donkey to mate with a mare on account of the revulsion he feels for her. In the Poitou region of France—which is the country's main centre of mule breeding—various techniques have been devised to make the donkey do his 'duty'.[8] One method is to sprinkle the urine of a female donkey in heat on the ground around the mare to make the mule think he is being taken to his normal partner. To deceive him the more easily, the encounter is usually arranged in the dark. The most effective method, however, we are told, is to play violin music for the donkey—or if a violinist is not available accordion music—to persuade him to 'co-operate'.

A proverb has it that it is impossible, and indeed contrary to nature, for a mule to procreate, but this is not altogether true: the male, it is true, is always sterile, but the female is occasionally fertile. The same applies to the cross of a stallion and a female donkey—the hinny. The male progeny of such a union is sterile while the·female is not.

However, to produce offspring, both the female mule and hinny alike must be crossed with a male horse or donkey, as the case may be, and not with a male of their own kind. This biological phenomenon is due to the fact that while female hybrids can produce normal eggs, the male can never produce viable spermatozoa.

The hinny lacks the stamina of the mule, and little effort is therefore made to breed this hybrid. On the other hand, the mule's modest fodder consumption and his sure-footedness in mountain terrain have ensured his success. Nowadays, however, due to the mechanisation of agriculture, the mule is becoming an increasingly rare sight. Before closing this chapter, we must not forget to mention another curious detail: the hinny neighs, while the mule brays: in other words, this would seem to be a rare instance of the father's influence counting for more than the mother's.

There is another domesticated member of the *Equidae* family—not a hybrid this time but a local breed of a species which exists in large numbers in Asia: the Tibetan Kiang, which is used as a pack animal and which in addition, serves man in another way: its dung is used for fuel.

*   *   *

The world's largest land animal has also been mastered by man. The domestication of the elephant began in India towards the end of the third millennium B.C. Throughout history, the Asian species has been far more used by man than the African, which is a good deal harder to train.

Elephants are used for a variety of tasks, e.g. they are employed for tiger hunting, but also—and above all—for hauling tree trunks in timber plantations. To capture elephants, the Indians drive wild herds into an enclosure called a corral. Once an animal has calmed down, it is handed over to two 'teacher' elephants who, traitors to their kind, persuade the newcomer to submit to domestication.

It is the prodigious strength of the animal which makes it so useful: an elephant can carry a load of 600 kg and work seven hours a day. Moreover, it can be taught perfect obedience to its *mahout*.

During the reign of the Indian Maurya dynasty, in the fourth century B.C., a curious technique was employed to train elephants. After an animal had been captured, its trunk, immobilised by having a strip of wood strapped to it, was attached to its tail by a rope which passed underneath the body. The elephant was then given a head-dress and collar, while a carpet with a geometrical design and bells at the corner was placed on its back. Finally, a long ribbon would be hung round its neck, with the two ends falling to knee height: once the animal began to move its knees would knock against the bells tied to the ribbon.

Man very soon began to use elephants in warfare—first in India and later in other countries. From the seventeenth century B.C. onward, war elephants were exported from India to the Middle East. Thus, in the fourth century B.C., Prince Sandracottus offered 500 elephants to his son-in-law Seleucus I Nicator, the founder of the Kingdom of Syria. The animals were later to prove of great value in the victorious battle he fought at Ipsus. The successors of Seleucus I continued to breed elephants at Apamea, in the Orontes valley.

The Indian King Porus also owned these 'living tanks'. When the army of Alexander the Great came face to face with the forces of Porus, the latter was struck by numerous arrows and thrown off his elephant. According to legend, the animal thereupon pulled the arrows out of Porus' body and lifted him back into the saddle, but soon the elephant itself was hit. As it collapsed—so we are told—it took care not to crush its master.

In the fourth and third centuries, most Asian armies used elephants. In a war against Darius III, King of Persia, Alexander is said to have captured fifteen elephants in the battle of Arbela and a dozen more at Susa. He later sent some of the animals to Aristotle in order that the illustrious philosopher might examine these creatures, which at that time were still virtually unknown to Europeans.

In the third century a new species—the African elephant—made its debut on the field of battle. The Egyptians were the first to domesticate the African elephant under the reign of Ptolemy II

Philadelphos. At that time, elephants still lived on the borders of Egypt, and special ranges were set aside for them on the Red Sea coast.

The battle of Raphia, in which the Asian elephants of Antiochus the Great met the African elephants of Ptolemy IV, proved a historic turning point. This was the first encounter between the two species—and it was hardly a friendly one ... The Egyptian pachyderms were put to flight by their Asian cousins. Their rout, however, did not prevent Ptolemy from gaining victory.

It was not long before Rome was confronted with the military threat posed by the elephant. In 280 B.C., Pyrrhus, King of Epirus, landed in Lucania with a force of elephants he had obtained from India. At the sight of these huge beasts the Roman troops took to their heels, scared by the 'Lucanian oxen', as they called them. The invader won several victories, which later, however, turned out to have been 'Pyrrhic' indeed. Finally defeated, the King abandoned a considerable number of his elephants to the Consul Curius Dentatus.

*   *   *

This was by no means the last encounter that Rome was destined to have with the elephant. For several decades, a city on the African coast was to make the Roman hearts tremble. That city, Carthage, twice sent its elephants into battle against Rome.

There were elephants in ancient times not only in Egypt but also in the Maghrib. The breed in question, it seems, was a good deal smaller than the elephant of tropical Africa. The Carthaginians established a vast elephant range on the narrows of the peninsula on which their city was sited.

In his novel *Salammbô*, Flaubert gives a masterly description of a battle in which the elephants of Carthage were involved:

> The soldiers were barely in possession of their arms; they had taken up their positions at random. They were frozen with terror; they stood undecided.
>
> Javelins, arrows, phalaricas, and masses of lead were already being showered down upon them from the towers. Some clung to the fringes of the caparisons in order to climb up, but their hands were struck off with cutlasses and they fell backwards

upon the swords' points. The pikes were too weak and broke, and the elephants passed through the phalanxes like wild boars through tufts of grass; they plucked up the stakes of the camp with their trunks, and traversed it from one end to the other, overthrowing the tents with their breasts. All the Barbarians had fled. They were hiding themselves in the hills bordering the valley by which the Carthaginians had come.[9]

Despite the fact that they had a force of elephants at their disposal, the Carthaginians lost the First Punic War. The surprise occasioned by the elephants of which Pyrrhus had been able to take advantage was by then a thing of the past. The Romans hurled flaming torches at the animals which, frightened out of their wits, turned on their own army. The commander of the latter thereupon gave orders to kill the beasts. The surviving elephants—142 in number—were captured by the Consul Metellus, who included them in his triumphal procession. Later, after the Senate had ordered them to be put to death, they were gathered in a circus arena and killed with bows and arrows.

Before long the Carthaginian army under the command of Hannibal again attacked Rome. In 218 B.C. Hannibal left for southern Spain at the head of nearly six thousand men and a force of fifty elephants. To reach Rome, his army first had to cross the Pyrenees and then the Alps—a great feat for animals from Africa. By the time they had got across the Pyrenees only thirty-seven of the elephants were still alive.

At Caderousse, south of Orange, Hannibal's army crossed the Rhône. The historian Polybius has left us a description of this episode. The Carthaginians first built rafts which they covered with soil and grass turves, to make the elephants feel at home. Ships then towed the rafts to the opposite bank. The elephants were at first scared when they realised they were floating upon water, and a number of them threw themselves into the Rhône, but got away with a ducking and managed to gain the bank.

To this day, tourists can see the holes where the posts to which the rafts were tied had been fixed. A 'Hannibal Fountain' and a rock known as 'Hannibal's Elephant' remind us of this famous crossing of the Rhône. The passage across the Alps called for even greater courage, for the elephants were apt to slip on the ice and to fall into ravines. By the time Hannibal had reached the Plain of the River Po he had only eight elephants left. Nevertheless, he won several victories over the Romans, who at one time thought their city was about to fall.

But Hannibal's audacious enterprise, just like the first one, met with failure and of his elephants only a single one survived to return to the range at Carthage: this seasoned warrior had fought six battles against the Romans. Later, war elephants were to see service in Numidia (which corresponds in part to the present-day Algeria), but it was not long before they finally disappeared from the West.

In Asia, on the other hand, elephants remained in military use until quite recently. In the seventeenth and eighteenth centuries, the Kings of Java, the Indian and Burmese Princes and the Mogul Emperors constantly used elephants, as did the British army in India. In Thailand, elephants were in great demand until the last century. In 1856, a King of Thailand owned no fewer than 800 elephants, which were divided into three groups according to the tasks they had to perform: one group hauled supplies; the second carried the King and his men, while the third group—an elite corps of 400 elephants—was used in battle as a shock force. The elephants attached to the infantry carried a turret on their backs in which sharpshooters were placed. Other elephants served the artillery; they carried platforms with light guns on them.

Indifferent to danger, the Siamese elephants charged the enemy with courage, and they were remarkably mobile. Their heads, trunks and other vulnerable parts were protected with sheets of 'armour' made of heavy rubber. It was as recently as 1882 that these elephants were last used in battle.

In the last century both the Thais and the Cambodians revered the white elephant. Whenever an albino elephant was discovered, a palace and a team of servants would be set aside for it. The animal would be covered with precious stones, pearls and golden bangles. The white elephant was thought to embody the soul of Buddha. To this day, the animal is also featured in Thailand's coat of arms. The luxury with which white elephants were surrounded recalls the great state in which the sacred bull Apis was kept in ancient Egypt.

As for the African elephant, people lost interest in it—or perhaps we should say left it in peace—in the nineteenth century. But in 1880, missionaries in Gabon succeeded in domesticating the animal, and in 1927 a centre for training elephants was set up at Gangala-Na-Bodio, in the north-eastern part of what was then the Belgian Congo—the present-day Zaire. The methods used were those developed in Asia. Thanks to this centre, there were some fifty domesticated elephants in the Congo in 1954.

Since then, however, all attempts to 'master' the African elephant have to all intents been abandoned. To sum up, in view of the sheer size of the beast, the domestication of the elephant must be seen as a great human achievement. This is what we should remember when we see a string of elephants in the circus ring, each holding on with its trunk to the tail of the one in front. Incidentally, elephant shows in the circus are no recent innovation: the Romans even managed to make elephants walk on a tight-rope!

This is how Pliny the Elder described such a scene: 'Then they even walked a tight-rope . . . It is one of the most astonishing sights to see them climb a rope and then descend it again, all the more so as they perform this feat head first.' Suetonius, too, has left us a description of such a performance: 'A well known Roman nobleman, sitting on an elephant, descended a rope.' He goes on to say that the Emperor Galba, included in 'the Floralia Festival which he gave during his tenure a display by tight-rope dancing elephants (*elephantos funambulos*), a spectacle never before seen'. And Seneca wrote: 'A tiny Ethiopian makes an elephant go down on his knees and walk a rope.' How can we possibly disbelieve such eminent witnesses?

[1] This word is pronounced *Pottyok*; the plural is *Pottokak*, pronounced *Pottyoka*.

[2] Pronounced *Pshevalski*.

[3] The chthonic world is the interior of the earth.

[4] The Shamans are the witch doctors of Central and Northern Asia.

[5] The *avâtara* of Vishnu are the ten incarnations of this god.

[6] Translated by Leonard Tancock, Penguin Books, 1954.

[7] *Découvrir les Animaux*, No. 70, p. 1, 14 July 1971.

[8] See the amusing study by M. Valière; 'L'acte de naissance du mulet du Poitou: le brelandage', *Bulletin folklorique d'Ile-de-France,* 4ᵉ série, No. 8, 1969, pp. 172–6.

[9] Translated by J. C. Chartres, Everyman's Library.

CHAPTER SEVEN

Small Mammals

LET US now pass from the largest domesticated mammal to the small ones. Of these, one is of outstanding importance: the rabbit. It is descended quite simply from the wild rabbit, well known to sportsmen and foresters and, of course, not particularly popular with the latter.

The species originates from the Iberian Peninsula, where it was discovered by the Roman Legions towards the beginning of the first century B.C. Later it spread to all parts of Europe including Britain. The Romans very soon domesticated the wild rabbit and bred it in special enclosures.

While the domesticated rabbit's wild ancestor is to this day grey, the domesticated varieties, thanks to selection, sport a great variety of colours. As well as being a source of meat, they provide us with pelts: the 'Rex' breeds of rabbit have the characteristic of being free of coarse hair, their coat consisting entirely of soft fur. This peculiarity is in fact the result of a disease which first struck rabbit farms around

Man and Animal : interdependence and mutual affection here beautifully illustrated in this painting by Maksimovic Borivos.

Spanish 15th-century lustred and painted plate with deer.

A Sassanian silver dish showing King Shapur II hunting astride a stag (4th century).

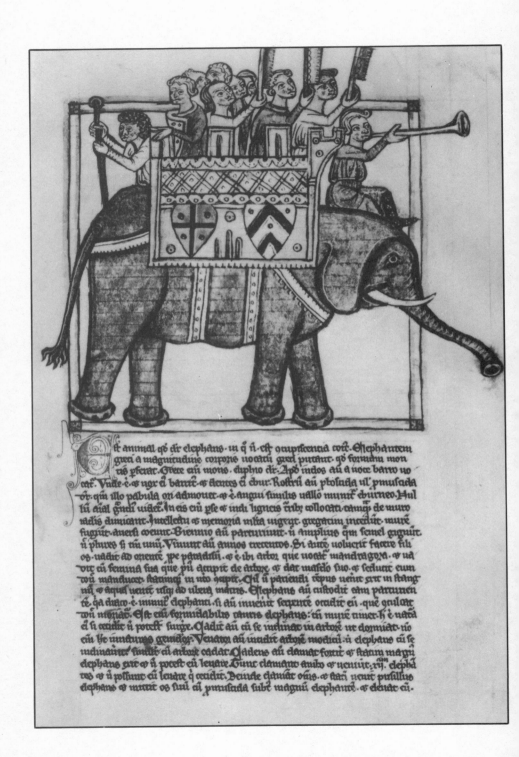

The elephant is one of man's most useful, long-lived and intelligent friends
(13th-century English bestiary).

The most treasured possessions of the legendary King Hilar of India were these three elephants, two riding camels and this splendid thoroughbred horse (Hümayunname, 16th century).

St George, patron saint of England and Byzantium from a 17th-century Ethiopian manuscript.

13th-century Northumberland knight on horseback, on a utensil for washing hands at table.

(below) 350 B.C. Thessalian Goddess Hecate with horse and dog; (centre) Sioux shield cover; (below right) West African camels and mules used in trade.

The sacred bull and crane adorn the Mycenaean pottery bowl *(above)* from Cyprus (1300 B.C.); *(below):* a delightful pair of Japanese Netsuke rabbits.

In this Turkish 16th–century manuscript, villagers marvel at the tortoise who is borne by his two duck friends as the trio could not be parted (Hümayunname).

Man's devotion to his domesticated anima[...]
deification: *(left)* Northwest Coast Indian [...]
religious falcon's head; *(below left)* 30 B.C. Ro[...]
mummified [...]

been transformed into *left)* 850 B.C. Egyptian ian bronze cat; *(right)* ian cat.

Nazca Indian bird pot.

Peruvian gold and silver alpaca *(above)* and llama *(opposite)*. Both have been domesticated by the Inca for millenia and are regarded as sacred friends. Alpaca wool is highly prized and the Inca weave their marvellous cloths from it and llama wool. The llama is also a deft mountain pack-animal.

INDIAN
ANIMAL

Recuay warrior and llama.

A fantasy incorporating domestic birds by the American painter Morris
Hirshfield.

1924. Perhaps we should also mention the splendid Angora rabbit, famous for its long hair. The breeders have even managed to produce a small white rabbit intended for use by magicians: it is just the right size for their top hats! Nowadays, the rabbit has started a new career—that of domestic pet.

The rabbit is no longer classed as a rodent but as a member of the small order of Lagomorpha. There are, however, true domestic rodents, principally the guinea-pig and the hamster.

The guinea-pig is neither a pig nor is it from Guinea: it hails, in fact, from the Andean Cordillera and owes its name to the ancient confusion between America and India. The word guinea-pig has become virtually synonymous with 'laboratory animal' *tout court*—a connection which the guinea-pig would probably gladly have done without. At all events, it quite clearly prefers the role of domestic pet, one which it has come to play more and more. The guinea-pig was first domesticated by the Incas before the Spanish conquest. They ate it, and sacrificed it to their gods—during the summer, for example, to make sure of a good harvest. The species was first imported into Europe in the sixteenth century.

The golden hamster, which has been much in fashion for the last ten years, has a very curious history. The fact is that all hamsters throughout the world are cousins, descended from a single pregnant female found in Syria about 1920. She belonged to the species 'Golden Hamster', which had spread as far westward as Rumania, but this particular specimen had a peculiar characteristic: she was 'erythric', i.e. she was a mutant with a marked prevalence of reddish hair. No other such specimen has ever been seen since. The golden hamster must not be confused with the Common Hamster, which has a black abdomen and inhabits the plains of Europe, from Alsace to Russia.

The white mouse, which is an albino mutant of the grey mouse, is a much-loved pet, although some people find it somewhat repulsive. Similarly, the white rats bred in laboratories are an albino variant of the brown rat.

Other rodents and carnivores are bred for their pelts. Now extremely rare in its original home, the Andes, the chinchilla has long been in great demand for this very purpose: even the Incas used to weave cloth from its wool. Subsequently, trackers killed the animals wholesale and all but exterminated it. In France, there are at present some 500 chinchilla breeders, with a breeding stock of about 5,000 females.

Two large aquatic rodents are also bred in Europe for their pelts. One is the musk rat or Ondatra, which has come to us from North America. Unfortunately, about 1927 a number of specimens managed to escape from captivity and have since spread right across Europe. Today, musk rats abound in the marshes of northern France: their lodges indicate their presence. Theirs is an addition to wild life that people would gladly have done without, for the musk rat causes considerable damage.

The coypu originates from South America, and, like the musk rat, has also reverted to the wild state in Europe. It is, however, much less widespread than the latter. In France, there are some twenty breeders, who own a breeding stock of 400 in all. The coypu is also known as nutria and myocastor—a fairish number of names for a single animal!

Several types of carnivores are bred on farms for their pelts, e.g. the sable, bred in Siberia, and the skunk, with its black-and-white fur, which can be found on hundreds of farms in the United States. However, the most important carnivores in this category are the mink and the silver fox.

The mink is widespread in the wild state, both in America and in Europe and Asia. The wild mink is invariably chestnut-coloured all over, but domesticated variants have been bred sporting a range of colours: there are white, silver and fawn ones.

The silver fox is a variety found in particularly large numbers in North America. The white and black hairs of its coat are closely intermingled; only the point of the tail is all-white.

In 1890, the first silver fox farm was established on an island in the estuary of the St. Lawrence River in Canada. Later, other farms were set up in the United States, Norway, Sweden, the U.S.S.R., etc. The Arctic Fox, which turns all white in the winter, is also bred in Norway. The 'Blue Fox' is a rare variety, with a greyish-blue coat.[1]

During the last war, some French prisoners of war in Germany were put to work on fox farms. One of them was Father Gervais Dumeige, now Professor at the Gregorian University in Rome. At our request, he gave us this account of his unusual experience:

> I spent more than four years of my life working with silver and blue foxes. While a prisoner of war I was,

like so many of my comrades, hired out as a farm labourer. After a spell of hard physical toil, chance decided that I should work on a fox farm. It occupied 20 hectares of Pomeranian sand, on which batteries of cages measuring either 5 by 5 or 5 by 8 metres were ranged. In all, there were 10,000 animals on the farm. They had to be cared for and fed with a mash which varied in composition and quantity according to the day of the week and the size of the animal. The foxes also had to be watered—up to three times a day in summer—and occasionally a disinfectant would be added to their drink as a precaution against the spread of disease. Every day their cages had to be cleaned out and any animal that had not eaten its food was reported.

The prisoners would look after their foxes from birth to death—and sometimes even from before birth. During the mating season, the entire farm was utterly silent. The animals were left together in pairs and the mating was watched from an observation post. Once the mating season was over, the females would be removed and allowed to carry their progeny, the period of gestation being 52 days. During that time, the vixens would pull out hair from their ruffs to line their nests. On the farm, however, instead of burrows the animals had boxes where they lived in strict seclusion, as if afraid of being disturbed. The litters, up to five for a silver fox and seven for a blue fox, were divided into cages in lots of three or four. There they would fight over their food, which they would try to bury—in vain, since the floor of the cages consisted of stout wire netting.

At that stage, the cubs had not yet finished growing, and the time came when each little fox had to be given its own cage, where it ate, drank and slept—as a rule showing a fair degree of hostility towards the person who came to clean its cage. At feeding time, the whole farm reverberated with the noise the foxes made as their food was brought in little trucks on rails. As the vehicles with their food pails approached, the foxes stamped their feet on the little shelves on which the food was about to be deposited. They gulped down their hash greedily and what they could not eat right away they stored in a corner of the cage. At the height of the summer the food would be frizzled by the pitiless sun, but it may well have tasted all the better for it. In mid-summer fifteen horses would be killed each day to provide food for the foxes. The big horse bones, boiled in a giant cauldron, made a soup which was greatly appreciated by the foxes, while the main course consisted of minced meat, mashed up with yeast, potatoes and occasionally dried milk (at the height of a war!). There were always a few bones left in the hash, but this did not worry the foxes, with their strong, sharp teeth.

I could tell many a tale about the foxes' teeth! More than one prisoner was bitten, for, when a beast was to be examined it first had to be grabbed by the tail and then by one leg, and finally stretched out on a flat surface. The keeper concerned had to hold the fox with one hand by the neck, otherwise it would turn over and seize its captor with its teeth and refuse to let go until the keeper first relaxed his grip.

Each fox had its own register number consisting of four digits, as well as a letter tattooed on one ear. The males were given even numbers and the females odd. Occasionally, the foxes would suffer from earache, and when that happened the prisoners of war had to clean out the animal's ears. Before the start of the operation the men carefully tied up the fox's lower jaw, and during the treatment they made sure the fox did not tear the string with a paw. Beasts which refused to eat were given vitamin B injections. They could not have been looked after better!

If a female blue fox had trouble whelping, the offspring had to be assisted into this world by means of a Caesarian section. Care was taken that the room where the operation was carried out was at a constant temperature of 36°. Since in such cases the cubs could not be suckled by their mother, cats were used as wet nurses. They treated the fox cubs exactly as they did their kittens. In the summer, the animals had to be combed to ensure good fur growth in the winter. This operation, which was done with a copper comb, was repeated again and again to remove any matted fur, for this might have interfered with the breathing of the skin and the formation of new fur.

At the end of the autumn a group of officials would arrive from Berlin to select the foxes to be culled during the following winter. On the fateful day, an end would be put to the fox's life with an injection into the heart. Every day, 400 animals would be destroyed in this way. This went on until Christmas, by which time the stock would be down to 2,000 head. The surviving animals were retained for breeding.

Can foxes be domesticated? I have seen a female blue fox which, adopted at a very young age and looked after throughout by the same person, became so familiar with its owner that it would recognise him by his smell. At his approach the fox would lie flat on the ground, its tail wagging, apparently full of joy. As a rule, however, the foxes seemed to distrust people instinctively. On the other hand, they undoubtedly grew accustomed to a 'domestic' life of sorts, to meals served at regular times, etc., and this regime cancelled out some of their predatory instincts.

When the Red Army liberated Eastern Germany, it also entered Zechendorf, the village where the fox farm was situated. The Russian soldiers opened the cages and let the foxes go. Since liberation was what it was all about, why not liberate everybody? However, the foxes found nothing to eat outside their cages and proved incapable of fending for themselves in freedom, and so they returned to their cages of their own accord, for this is where they were used to finding nourishment.

Why did the Germans raise foxes in the middle of a war? The farm, which had originally belonged to some Jewish fur merchants, had been nationalised and the Third Reich sold the pelts to its allies for foreign currency. Who would have believed that employment on a fox farm would be classed as war work?

My work with foxes made me something of an expert. Back in France, I one day stopped outside a fur shop and, on being asked ironically by the owner how it came about that a priest was so interested in furs. I remarked that the goods in his shop window were not all that might be desired from the point of view of quality. I explained to him the exact technical reasons why I thought this to be the case. The furrier was dumbfounded by so much expertise on the part of a priest. As for the former fox farmer, he went back to his theology books.'

An American animal, the opossum, is also bred for its fur. Lastly, in Ethiopia, the civet is kept in captivity, but for a different reason: the secretion of its musk glands is collected. Docile beasts that they are, civets readily present their glands, which are situated close to the anus, to the breeders!

[1]A number of finds seem to indicate that small foxes were already domesticated at the time of the lake settlements.

CHAPTER EIGHT

The Birds

BIRDS ACCOUNT for many of the species of animal life domesticated by man. They can be divided into two categories: first, those kept for purely utilitarian ends—i.e. the various types of farmyard poultry; secondly, there are the birds which are kept for ornamental purposes in parks, on lakes or ponds, in cages or aviaries.According to Jean Dorst, professor at the National Museum of Natural History in Paris, the various species of domestic birds were originally gregarious and vegetarian. The only exception to this rule are the hunting birds (falcons), and the fishing birds (cormorants), which we have already mentioned. Their domestication, however, is of a different order.

The most important domesticated bird is obviously the domestic fowl. It is descended from the South-East Asian species *Callus bankiva*, which was domesticated about 2500 B.C. This feat was achieved by the people of the Indus Valley civilisation, one of the oldest known. From this region, the domestic fowl spread both east and westward, reaching Egypt in the sixteenth century B.C. and China in the fourteenth.

During the first millennium B.C. a further expansion took the domestic fowl via Persia to Central Europe, where it found a home in the sixth century B.C. Thanks to selection, the number of breeds has grown remarkably: at present there are more than 200. There are chickens with bare necks, others have feathers all the way down the legs, and there is even a breed which has six claws. In Japan there is a cock whose tail grows by 1 metre a year to a maximum of 6 metres.

The cock has always played a role of immense importance in mythology and folklore, the arts and literature. The Tassili frescoes include a picture of two men and a cock perched on a structure whose nature has remained a mystery, while certain Babylonian sculptures depict priests in the act of prayer, facing a cock. There would appear to be a common theme here which is worthy of note.

In Egypt the cock was associated with the secret cult of Thoth; in Persia, every family kept a cock, whose crowing wakened the people at dawn. It is mainly for his voice that the bird is famous. At the death of Cecrops, the legendary founder of Athens, a number of cocks were sacrificed on his grave and, according to legend, Cecrops rose up from the dead, though in the form of a lion. Despite being the symbol of resurrection, vigilance and vitality, the Greeks nevertheless sacrificed the cock to Thanatos, i.e. Death. The dying Socrates made this request of Kriton: 'We owe Asclepios for a cock. Well then, settle my debt, bear it in mind.' Those were the philosopher's last words. He may have been following an ancient tradition, for the cock was also the symbol of the immortality of the soul.

Ancient legend has shrouded the cock with an air of mystery. The Greeks associated the bird with Hermes Trismegistus, who was the Greek equivalent of, and identical with, Thoth: Hermes was considered to be the founder of alchemy, which was thus the 'Hermetic' science *par excellence*. Some light was shed on the symbolic role of the cock by the Greek author Lucian of Samosata in the second century A.D. in his dialogue *The Dream or the Cock*. One of the characters in the dialogue is a cock who is both a reincarnation of Pythagoras and a companion of Hermes—once again we have here an allusion to the link between Hermes and the cock. A Greek *bas-relief* depicts the sacrifice of a cock to Bellona, the goddess of war.

In China the cock is regarded as a symbol of good fortune, thanks to the fact that the words for 'cock' and 'luck' are one and the same: *Ki*. To the Chinese the cock is also the protector of the family, and there are many representations of the bird showing it in the act of killing a scorpion or a millipede. In India, too, the cock is regarded as a portent of good fortune. Among the ancient Chaldaeans, the cock was the object of a curious belief: it was thought that each morning the cock—and the cock alone—receives a divine inspiration from the planet Mercury which reaches no one else since at that time all the other creatures are still fast asleep. It was the belief in this divine influence which was at the root of the custom of dedicating the cock to Hermes-Thoth.

The Moslems believe that each morning a sacred cock sings a paean of glory in honour of Allah and that its ordinary earthly counterparts merely repeat the holy bird's song. The same tradition once existed among the Scandinavians, who believed that the red cock Fjalar sings in Valhalla and that it is his crowing which announces the coming of the Sun, which they worshipped.

In Rome, the cock played an important part in the art of soothsaying. Political decisions were based on the appetite of the sacred fowl, and certain priests, the Augurs, claimed to be able to predict the future by this means. Cicero, however, questioned the validity of such predictions. Pliny the Elder believed that the crowing of the cock frightened lions away, while Lucretius went so far as to claim that the eyes of felines were liable to be struck by atoms emanating from the bird. Ovid tells of a cock being sacrificed to the Goddess of the Night—no doubt because he disturbed her rest with his crowing.

In many Christian countries, and notably in France, church steeples are crowned with weathercocks. According to a legend, St. Peter, full of anger at the cock since it reminded him of his denials of Christ, impaled it and placed it where it could be seen by all men. This was said to be the origin of the weathercock but, in fact, the first weathercock was probably put up in the year A.D. 800 at Brescia, in Italy, and another is definitely known to have been in use in 1091 at Coutances in Normandy. An early weathercock—that of Westminster Abbey—is depicted on the famous Bayeux Tapestry.

According to an obstinate belief, which maintained itself from the days of classical antiquity until as late as the seventeenth century, the cock is gifted with the power of putting ghosts to flight. It was a cock which, on the battlements of Elsinore Castle, caused the ghost of

Hamlet's father to vanish, and Shakespeare makes Horatio say:

> I have heard
> The cock, that is the trumpet to the morn,
> Doth with his lofty and shrill-sounding throat
> Awake the god of day; and at his warning,
> Whether in sea or fire, in earth or air,
> Th' extravagant and erring spirit lies
> To his confine; and of the truth herein
> This present object made probation.

In days gone by the good people of Prague used to sacrifice a cock at the Cathedral of St. Vitus to the saint of that name in order to cast out the spells put on them by the devil. The ancestors of the present-day Czechs had long before that greatly feared the God Swantwit, and it was in his honour that they originally used to offer up the bird. St. Vitus, or *Sanctus Vitus* in Latin, was popularly known as *Sanc With,* a name which sounded very similar to that of the old god Swantwit—hence the confusion between the saint and the god.

In the Poitou region of France, a popular custom persists to this day whereby a woman is required to cut the throat of a black hen in the fireplace and to sprinkle its blood in front of the door of a newly-built house. It is said that failure to do this will result in a bereavement in the owner's family. In the West Indies, people will to this day sacrifice a black cock to persuade a genie to use his influence with a trial judge. In Liberia, a cock—though a white one for a change—is sacrificed to mark the visit of an honoured guest.

The famous 'Gallic cock' has been the subject of much controversy. According to some theories, the Gauls in fact never really venerated the cock. We are told that it is all a case of verbal confusion since the Latin word *Gallus* stands for both 'cock' and 'Gaul'. This, we are told, is at the root of the custom of honouring the Gallic cock, which dates from the latter part of the fifteenth century. But on the other hand there are those who staunchly maintain their partisanship of the Gallic cock. They argue that cocks made of baked clay dating from the time of the Gauls have been discovered (examples can be seen at the museum in Saint-Germain-en-Laye, near Paris) and also that poultry bones dating from the second century A.D. have been found in burial pits in the Vendée. This, they maintain, proves that the cock played an important part among the people of Gaul. Chantecler, the cock in the ancient *Roman de Renart*, took his role as protector of hens very seriously. He was immortalised by Edmond Rostand in his famous play of the same title (1910).

The alchemists regarded the cock as the symbol of natural heat emanating from Mercury. Among the Buddhists, the Wheel of Tibetan civilisation has three animals at its hub: the serpent, the pig and the cock, the latter symbolising sexual passion.

Two pastimes in one case depended—and in the other still depend—on the cock. The first was cock-racing, which used to be practised in France. On Easter Monday the squire of Pons would lead a procession from house to house and knock on every door to demand the payment of a live cock. As soon as he had got his bird, the squire's bailiff would throw it up into the air. The bird would of course try to get away as fast as it could and the crowd chased it in hot pursuit across the fields. If the bird tried to cross a river, its pursuers would jump in after it . . . This custom disappeared at the time of the Revolution in 1789.

The other pastime is much more widespread in terms of both space and time—and it is also more controversial. We are referring, of course, to the famous sport of cockfighting, which exploits the bird's combative qualities. Cockfighting was very much in fashion during classical antiquity, when it was also used as a means of predicting the future. Cicero and Pliny have left us descriptions of such fights, which are also depicted in a mosaic in Pompeii.

The cocks used for fighting in classical antiquity were closely related to the Indian *Gallus bankiva*, but the Malay fighting cock, which can be found throughout Malaysia and Indonesia, is of even more ancient lineage. It is used—armed with spurs—in the Philippines, where it had its greatest vogue in the last century. The Malay fighting cock was also introduced into Europe, where it became known as the 'English fighting cock'. Cockfighting was extremely popular in England under Henry II and Elizabeth I, but then went into something of a decline. It may have been under the impact of the Spanish occupation—and there is surely a parallel between cockfighting and bullfighting—that the pastime became fashionable in Flanders, where it has remained popular to this day. The Flemish fighting cocks owe more to the *bankiva* than to the Malay breed. Cockfighting is also practised in the West Indies, Mexico, Colombia and Peru, but has lost some of its popularity in these areas. The custom even extends as far as Polynesia. In Mexico, fighting cocks are drugged with Indian hemp . . .

Before the beginning of a bout, the cock has to be 'groomed'. In Flanders, comb and wattles are trimmed to offer the minimum hold to the adversary, and most of the tail feathers are also cut. In Colombia, a horizontal strip is trimmed across the underside of the bird's body; the bare skin thus exposed to the sun hardens to form a natural 'shield'.

The main armament however, which multiplies the cock's fighting power tenfold, are his spurs. In Flanders the spurs are fixed to the bird's heels, which are split when the bird is old enough to be put out in a run. The spurs used in northern France are straight, conical, metal spikes, about 5 cm long, attached to a ring which is strapped to the leg by a leather thong.

The 'weapons' of fighting cocks have varied over the centuries and from region to region. The Greeks used to place a pointed metal 'cap' over the bird's heel. In Scotland, weapons made of ivory were used; in South America curved spikes are the chosen weapon, while in Mexico preference is given to flat blades sharpened at the two edges. Supporters of the sport believe that fighting between unarmed cocks is more cruel than bouts between armed birds. Nevertheless, the sport of cock fighting has aroused the indignation of animal lovers just as much as bullfighting. As long ago as the Middle Ages, an Archbishop of Bordeaux banned cockfighting on pain of ex-communication. The facts justify the claims of the sport's opponents since sixty per cent of the cocks used in this way are killed and twenty per cent permanently maimed.

Two other domesticated gallinaceous birds can often be found side by side with farmyard chickens: the turkey and the guinea-fowl. The first has come to us from the Indies—in this instance from the 'West Indies', i.e. America. Descended from the Mexican wild turkey, which was domesticated by the Indians well before the Spanish conquest, it was introduced into Europe in the sixteenth century. The first pair of these birds was offered as a present to the then Pope in 1523 by the Archbishop of Santo Domingo. However, it appears that it was not until 1571 that the first turkey was eaten in France—at the wedding of Charles IX.[1]

As for the guinea-fowl, it comes from Africa and was brought to Greece at the beginning of the fifth century B.C., but it was the Romans who introduced it to many of the regions of Europe. Two breeds domesticated on our continent since classical antiquity— the blue-wattled guinea-fowl and the red-wattled variety— subsequently both disappeared from Europe. The first is now only bred in Madagascar, while the second was reintroduced into Europe in the sixteenth century by Portuguese discoverers. Incidentally, the French name for the bird, *pintade*, comes from the Portuguese *pintado*, which means 'painted hen'. The guinea-fowl was also imported into the West Indies, where it reverted to the wild state.

*   *   *

Side by side with these three birds, two web-footed birds can be found in many farmyards: the duck and the goose. Most domesticated ducks are descended from the Mallard, a common European wild duck. The male has a green head and a white neck band. It appears that this species was domesticated independently at one and the same time in several regions of Eurasia, notably in Mesopotamia and China. It is from the latter that the Mandarin duck, with its white livery, has come to us. The ancient Teutons raised ducks from the Hallstatt period onward, i.e. since the iron age, but in the Mediterranean region the duck does not appear to have been domesticated until later.

The Muscovy or Barbary duck is quite distinct from the other breeds: it originates from South America, where it was domesticated by the Peruvian Indians. It was later introduced intoduced into Africa by the slave traders, and thence spread to Europe. In England, it was first bred during the reign of Henry VIII. This large bird is recognisable by its red caruncles, or wattles, between the bill and the eyes. plumage is a shiny metallic green with white spots. The bird has the habit, unique among ducks, of perching in trees. It readily mates with the various races of the Mallard.

The domestication of the goose dates way back from the Neolithic age and seems to have been accomplished first in South-Eastern Europe. The domestic goose is descended from the greylag, one of the European wild geese. According to Homer, Penelope owned a flock of geese, and it is the Greeks who invented the game which to this day is known in France as *'jeu de l'oie'*, or Goose Game. This—on the face of it—rather unexciting pastime is based on a profound symbolism, for it reflects man's progress as he makes his way laboriously through life's snares.

The story of the sacred geese which are said to have saved the Capitol by their cries during an attack by the Gauls in 388 B.C. shows that the Romans held the goose in high regard. Large flocks of geese used to be driven to Rome on foot across Gaul.

The importance of the goose was particularly great under the Merovingian dynasty: to the Franks, the goose was the symbol of the art of steel-making. The facts behind their belief are these: the Franks used to crush iron into small pieces, blend the latter with flour and feed this mix to their geese. The resulting droppings were used as a case-hardening agent in the forging of sword blades. This method was employed because of the abundance of carbon and nitrogen present in goose manure.

As with all farmyard poultry, the goose serves as a table bird, but it is prized especially for its *foie gras,* the enlarged liver which results from the somewhat cruel methods used in fattening the birds for this specific purpose. The Toulouse goose is thought to produce the best *foie gras*, a delicacy which has an ancient history, for the Romans were very fond of *foie gras*. In Paris, shops which specialised in selling roast goose meat were particularly numerous in a street which consequently became known as *Rue aux Oies*, or Goose Street. Subsequently this was distorted to *Rue aux Ours,* Bear Street. . .

Goose down, used in the manufacture of quilted coats, was once known by the misleading term of 'swan's down'. Literature owes a debt of gratitude to the goose because it was goose quills which writers used in their work. Quills imported from Switzerland, Italy, Germany and Russia were highly prized, while in France it was the geese from the Poitou region which were believed to provide the best quills.

Farmers used to pluck their geese three times a year. Each bird produced up to half a pound of feathers and just over one and a half ounces of down a year. In 1912, a kilo of feathers sold at eight to ten francs, and a kilo of down at fifteen francs.[2]

Several other types of geese have also been domesticated in the course of history. We shall return to these in the chapter about 'Forgotten Domestications'. One such breed, which comes from the Far East, can still be seen in our farmyards—the Chinese goose, the domesticated variety of which is mistakenly called in France *Oie de Guinée*. Its plumage is grey or spotted, and it has a caruncle. The breed was probably first domesticated in China, and from the Far East it spread to the Ukraine and even as far afield as Madagascar, A single district of that island was once estimated to contain no fewer than 300,000 head of these geese, which yield excellent meat. The Chinese goose readily mates with the common goose.

* * *

It is once again the ancient Egyptians to whom must go the honour of having domesticated a species of the first importance—the pigeon. This seems to have been accomplished towards 3000 B.C., under the Fourth Dynasty. From Egypt, the fashion of pigeon breeding soon spread to Greece and Rome. The Romans built dovecots on the roofs of their houses. Later the sport of pigeon-fancying spread simultaneously as far as India and Western Europe.

As Darwin has shown, the many breeds of domestic pigeon are all, or nearly all, descended from the rock dove. This species, characterised by grey wings with black bands, white tail feathers, iridescent neck feathers and coral-red legs, nests, as its name suggests, on rocks and cliffs. There was a time when it nested in considerable numbers along several stretches of the French coast, especially the mouth of the Seine, on the Belle-Ile and in Corsica. It has now disappeared from most of these parts, at least in its pure-bred form.

Under the impact of domestication and selection, the outward appearance of the pigeon has become much more varied. The runt pigeon can be up to 50 cm long, with a wing span of 1 metre. The better known fantail is entirely white and is able to spread its tail feathers to form a fan. Two other breeds are notable for their unusual characteristics: the Pouter pigeon, which dilates its crop by swallowing air so that its chest becomes the shape of a huge balloon; and the Tumbler pigeon, which does pirouettes in the air, almost certainly due to an anomaly which affects its organs of balance.

Hardly had the pigeon been domesticated when men began to take advantage of its extraordinary navigational skill. The carrier-pigeon might well claim to be descended from the biblical dove, which brought the famous olive branch back to Noah's Ark. Spiteful tongues maintain that this messenger could only have been a male, for no female could have kept its beak shut for that length of time! . . .

The first real carrier-pigeons appear in ancient Egypt: the Egyptians would launch them into the air from their ships. The use of the carrier-pigeon then spread to Phoenicia, Greece and Rome: in 43 B.C., Brutus, besieged in Modena by Mark Anthony, used carrier-pigeons to communicate with his allies, but it would seem that the honour of having created the first regular 'pigeon post' must go to the Emperor Diocletian.

Thereafter, the sport of pigeon-fancying underwent a prolonged decline in Europe, though it remained popular in Persia, Syria and Egypt: in the latter country, an air mail service was organised as far back as the twelfth century. The West rediscovered the carrier-pigeon at the time of the Crusades. In France the birds were then used to carry messages from *château* to *château* and monastery to monastery, and the possession of birds of prey, liable to worry the pigeons, was severely punished.

In 1573, William of Orange used carrier-pigeons during the siege of Haarlem in the Netherlands War of Independence. A little later, in 1590, the citizens of Paris, besieged by Henry IV, did likewise. During the eighteenth century, pigeon-fancying became firmly established in France, Britain and Germany. Pigeons kept the financiers of London informed of events in the Battle of Waterloo, thus assisting them in their speculations . . . In 1840, the journalist Reuter, the founder of the famous news agency of that name, set up a pigeon-post service between Verviers in Belgium and Aachen in Germany.

The best known episode in the history of pigeon keeping, however, occurred during the siege of Paris in 1870–1. Pigeons were released in the French capital to maintain a link with various provincial centres. To enable messages to be sent in the opposite direction, the pigeons were flown out of Paris by balloon beyond the encircling ring of Prussian troops. The first of these pigeons were put on board the balloon *Ville-de-Florence* on 25 September 1870.

Of the 363 pigeons released only seventy-three returned, and even so this figure of 'returns' included a number of birds which flew more than one mission. One hundred and fifty of the pigeons fell into the hands of the Prussians. The messages were attached to the birds' tail feathers; each message sheet, although a mere 30 by 55 mm, was a reproduction of twelve folio pages and contained anything up to 3,000 individual dispatches. The seventy-three 'returns' allowed 115,000 dispatches to be transmitted.

Carrier-pigeons also distinguished themselves in the two world wars. Mobile army dovecots were mounted on trailers or trucks. In the battle of Verdun, a pigeon carried the last message from Commandant Raynal, the defender of Fort Vaux. The bird died on arriving at its dovecot. After the 1914–18 war, several monuments were put up to honour the heroic carrier pigeons. Nowadays, pigeon fanciers are still particularly numerous in Belgium and Northern France.

* * *

The domestic fowl, the guinea fowl, the turkey, the duck, the goose and the pigeon are domestic birds in the true sense of the word, but there are also many species which are bred by man for less crudely utilitarian ends.[3] For example, some are used as ornamental birds in parks and gardens and on lakes and ponds. Such is the case of the mute swan. What sight can be more beautiful than a swan as it floats serenely through the limpid waters of a lake, its neck lightly arched and wings half open?

In the truly wild state, the species lives in the marshlands of Northern Europe. As one moves further north, beyond Schleswig-Holstein, one begins to see wild mute swans floating elegantly on the many lakes. In Western Europe, most of these swans live in a semi-wild state, while some are indeed wholly domesticated. Those on Lake Geneva are well known as are those on the Thames. In Britain swans used to be individually marked on the beak.[4] In Paris there is a causeway named in honour of the bird, the *Ile des Cygnes*, or Swan Island, in the Seine between the districts of Passy and Grenelle.

The swan has been kept as an ornamental bird only since the Middle Ages and increasingly since the Renaissance. The authors of classical antiquity speak only of the wild ancestor of our swan, which visits southern Europe in the winter.

Another species of the swan, the true wild swan, also spends the winter in Europe. It emits loud cries which may be the origin of the expression 'swan song', used to describe the last work of a writer or composer.

MAA

The swan has always symbolised grace: the swans of Aphrodite carried the light divine across Europe. Each year, Apollo would return to Greece on a chariot drawn by swans after staying with the Hyperboreans, the mythical inhabitants of Northern Europe. Castor and Pollux were hatched from an egg, thanks to the union of Leda and Zeus, the latter having assumed the shape of a swan for the purpose. In a German legend, Lohengrin floats down the river of life on a boat pulled by a swan. Some of the most elegant authors of literary history, such as Virgil and Fenelon, were known as 'swans'—the first 'the swan of Mantua' and the second as 'the swan of Cambrai'.[5] And while we are on the subject of the swan, how could we forget Hans Andersen's moving fairy-tale about the *Ugly Duckling*? Humiliated by its brothers because it was so plain, it turned into a majestic swan.

As well as the mute swan, two other species are occasionally found in parks. Of the two, the more popular is the Australian Black swan, which has a red bill. When brought to Europe, the Black swan from 'down under' at first retains its original 'biological time-clock' for several years, that is to say, the female lays her eggs when it is spring in Australia but autumn in the Northern Hemisphere. The rarer of the two species, the black-necked White swan, is also occasionally found on our lakes and ponds. This species comes from South America.

A large goose, with a white face contrasting with its black neck, the Canada goose, is also kept as a park bird, as is the Mandarin duck, with its resplendent plumage. This species originates from the Far East, and the habit of the male and female Mandarin of invariably swimming in pairs has led to the bird becoming the Chinese symbol of marital fidelity. The Mandarin duck also features prominently in Asian popular art, especially in pictures found in bedrooms.

If the swan is the ornament of ponds and lakes, the peacock is the ornament *par excellence* of the lawn. In the wild state, it lives in India and Indonesia. King Solomon's fleets are said to have brought back peacocks from these lands. The peacock was known in Europe at the time of Pericles, but it was only under Alexander the Great that it found a permanent home on our continent. The peacock became the bird of the Goddess Juno, and there were sacred peacocks at the temple of that goddess, on the Island of Samos. To this day, peacocks are kept in the grounds of temples and pagodas in India.

In Western Europe, however, the peacock was accepted only gradually, between the fourteenth and the seventeenth centuries. The fact is that while its plumage may be beyond compare, its piercing cry and the damage it does to crops can make it unwelcome: as a result, the fashion of keeping peacocks went into decline with the introduction of the turkey.

Nevertheless, the peacock is still greatly valued as an ornamental bird, and the sight of the male giving his display never loses its charm. There is also an albino variety—the White peacock. The fertility of the peacock has diminished over the centuries, while the reverse is true of most other domesticated birds.

The meat of the peacock, which is in fact far from appetising, was greatly appreciated in ancient Rome and even more so in the Western Europe of the Middle Ages. At banquets, the peacock would be carried in—its head and crest preserved in their original state—on a large platter escorted by a group of ladies and musicians.

In the Age of Chivalry, the peacock also played a ceremonial role: occasionally, a noble knight, with one arm raised above a peacock, would make a solemn vow. He might say, for example: 'I pledge myself before God, the Holy Virgin, the Ladies and the peacock to seize this town!'[6]

Several species of pheasant have been introduced into Europe. The best known is *Phasianus colchicus*, a splendid game bird which has become so widespread on our continent that it may now be regarded as in every way part and parcel of European bird life. Originally its habitat extended right across Asia, from the Caucasus to the China Sea, and it was brought to Europe from the shores of the Black Sea. The Romans released a number of pheasants in Corsica, and the bird was later taken from there to mainland Europe in the Middle Ages.[7] Among other varieties introduced into Europe one of the most outstanding is the Mongolian pheasant, whose most striking characteristic is a white neck band. In France, the breeding of pheasants developed in the seventeenth and eighteenth centuries.

Besides the varieties bred to stock game reserves, there are ornamental birds, such as the Golden pheasant; Lady Amherst's pheasant—a white, black and green bird which was imported into France under the reign of Napoleon III—and the Silver pheasant. This last bird, which has a white back and a black underside, is known to have been kept in a semi-domesticated state in the Far East for thousands of years, for it is featured on Chinese designs 5,000 years old. Let us finally mention Reeves' pheasant, the tail of which can be up to 2.40 metres in length.

All species of the pheasant originate from Asia.

*　　　*　　　*

Various types of birds are bred for their feathers—chief among them being the ostrich. Originally, this—the largest of all birds—was found in most parts of Africa, as well as the Middle East as far as Mesopotamia, but it became extinct in Asia in 1941.

The ancient Egyptians tried to breed the bird, and a number of tribes in the Sudan do in fact seem to have later succeeded with such attempts. In antiquity, a number of peoples are known to have existed in Ethiopia called *struthiophagi*, or 'ostrich eaters' (the Latin word *struthio* means ostrich).

However, it was mainly its magnificent plumes that excited attention. The Egyptians and Babylonians, and also the ancient kings of Brittany, made fans from ostrich plumes, and the latter were also much in evidence at the French Court for many centuries: King Henry IV's white-plumed helmet crest, for instance, was famous far and wide. Nowadays, however, ostrich plumes are only to be found on the cabaret stage. The fans, or *flabelli*, once used in the Vatican have recently been abolished.

At the suggestion of Geoffroy Saint-Hilaire, it was decided in 1860 in France to try to exploit the ostrich commercially. Experiments were made to this end in the Grenoble, Marseilles and Algiers zoos. Subsequently, domesticated ostriches were bred more widely—though often in a somewhat haphazard fashion—in North and Central Africa, Madagascar, Australia, Argentina, the U.S.A. and other countries; the only country, however, where commercial ostrich farming has really prospered is South Africa.

The ostriches are raised in a state of semi-freedom on enormous ranges. To encourage them to breed, their eggs are taken away and, as a result, the females will lay up to one hundred eggs a year instead of the normal total of about one dozen. The plumes are clipped to the root; a single ostrich can provide several thousand plumes in the course of its lifetime. Pedigree registers are kept to assist selection. In the past, people used to organise ostrich races, with the birds pulling small carts each carrying a driver.

In South America, repeated attempts have been made to breed the rhea, or nandu, the American cousin of the ostrich. In India, Pakistan and Tunisia people have experimented with breeding herons and egrets for their feathers. Along the Scandinavian coastline, the Eider duck—a large sea duck—nests in a semi-domesticated state close to areas of human habitation. People put out nesting boxes for the bird. The down, with which it lines its nest, is regularly removed and used in the manufacture of eiderdowns. This word, it hardly needs saying, is derived from the name of the bird. However, the Scandinavians do not only value the bird for its down but are also fond of eider eggs.

* * *

Numerous birds such as parrots, parakeets, turtle doves, canaries, budgerigars, etc., are kept in cages or aviaries.

The fashion of keeping parrots goes back to the days of classical antiquity. It is said that Alexander the Great brought back from India a ringed parakeet (*Palaeornis torquata*), a species which has therefore also been called Alexander's parakeet. The bird—whose plumage is green, with pink neck band—was greatly prized by the Greeks and Romans—so much so, in fact, that Cato severely criticised the exaggerated importance people were apt in those days to attach to the bird, a single specimen of which cost more than a slave.

The same species was known as 'popinjay' in the Middle Ages, when the gentry used to keep these birds in their castles. Many kings of France, from Charles V to Louis XIV, owned parrots. According to one story, once upon a time when a parrot which belonged to Henry VIII of England fell into the Thames, it called out, quite deliberately: 'Help, I am drowning!' We are told that thanks to its cries of distress the bird was indeed saved.

At the Castle of Schoenbrunn, the Empress Maria Theresa of Austria transformed a rococo pavilion into a 'parrot house'. In French literature, the bird was immortalised in Gresset's poem *Vert-Vert*, which tells about a wicked parrot that greatly shocked a group of nuns with the oaths it had learned on a sea voyage.

Parrots have throughout history been bred in India and China. Nowadays, they are sought after mainly for their ability to copy human speech. The variety most highly skilled in that respect is the pink-tailed African grey parrot. As long ago as 1780, a Governor of Senegal, the Chevalier de Boufflers, presented one of these creatures to Queen Marie Antoinette. The parrot has a rival in the mynah bird, a large Asian starling which is also a very good talker.

The budgerigar comes from Australia, whence it was first imported in 1840. Its plumage is green, but in addition breeders have produced blue, yellow, mauve, white and other varieties. The South American Indians are past masters of the art of producing parrots with, as it were, artificial plumage: they first pluck out a number of plumes and then smear the area thus bared with a product which acts on the *papillae* or roots of the plumes. As a result of this treatment, the new plumage takes on a different hue, for example yellow instead of blue.

Another bird often kept in aviaries is the laughing dove, which is descended from the Dove of Barbary, a pink and grey bird from tropical Africa. The laughing dove, which was highly prized by the Romans, is no relation of the true European wild doves—the turtle dove and the collared dove—although the latter resembles it closely.

The canary was brought to Europe from the islands after which it was named. It was probably domesticated there by the Guanches, the original inhabitants of the archipelago. In 1404, a French Baron, Jean de Bethencourt, 'Lord of the Canaries', presented some of these birds as a gift to the Court of Castile and later gave one to a Queen of France, Isabeau of Bavaria, wife of Charles VI.

The main centre of the canary trade in Europe was Genoa. In 1480, Louis XI bought more than 300 canaries. At that time, most of the bird shops of Paris were installed on a bridge, the Pont au Change. The owners tried in vain to impose a law prohibiting commoners from keeping canaries.

King Francis I established the post of 'Master of the Canary Birds' at his court; in addition there existed other offices, such as 'Feeder of the Nightingales' and 'Master of the Song Birds' . . . In the eighteenth century a new craft came into being, that of 'bird whistler', whose duty it was to give singing lessons to canary birds with the aid of recorders or flutes . . .

From then on, the canary went from strength to strength, so that today countless varieties exist.

Many other passerines are kept in cages, either as songbirds or because of the beauty of their plumage. The latter applies, for instance, to the South African Waxbill, which in French is called 'Bengali' although it comes in fact from Africa. This bird was first imported into Europe in the eighteenth century. The popularity of the passerines unfortunately meant that people took to catching these birds in huge numbers: alas, they are frequently kept in poor conditions.

European passerine birds should definitely not be kept in captivity. The practice is, in any case, prohibited as far as the majority of species is concerned. In the past, singing bird contests used to be held in Northern France and Belgium. The winner was the bird which repeated its own individual tune without a break more often than any other contestant. The cages were tied to a fence, and to each a small blackboard was attached with the bird's details written up in chalk, including the number of times the bird had repeated its particular song. In *Germinal,* Emile Zola describes such a competition, with deep-throated and high-pitched songsters trying to outdo one another. We need shed no tears over the passing of this custom.

Various other types of birds are kept in a more or less domesticated state in different parts of the world for a wide range of purposes. In South America, for instance, the duties normally performed by guard dogs are sometimes entrusted to the Agami, or trumpeter bird. The latter is related to the Rail and looks somewhat like a gallinaceous bird. The Agamis watch over the poultry. More rarely, the job is given to the Kamichi, or Horned screamer, a distant relation of the goose.

In New Guinea, the hornbill, well known for its enormous beak, lives in a state of semi-liberty in the Papuan villages. The birds quietly walk up and down between the rows of huts or else they obediently remain seated on a stick which their master carries over one shoulder.

The Asian peoples love the sport of quail fighting. This, however, is a misnomer since the birds involved are not quail but Turnix—birds which belong to the rail family, although they do in fact resemble the quail. A variety of the Turnix lives in Andalusia. The Turnix is remarkable in that it is an example of a rare phenomenon—sexual inversion—i.e. it is the female Turnix which,

as you might say, wears the pants! . . . The females, being pol-
yandrous, fight furiously for possession of the males. It is this
particular instinct which is put to use in 'quail fights' . . . Finally,
perhaps we should mention that the Afghans hold partridge fights.

[1] It was a turkey which, with an unfortunately aimed blow of its beak, is said to
have condemned Boileau to enforced permanent abstinence . . .

[2] In addition to goose quills, quills from swans, pelicans, cranes and vultures were
also used for writing.

[3] Let us mention, too, the hatcheries where quail, partridge, mallards and other
game-birds are bred to keep the shoots stocked. People also breed hares for this
purpose.

[4] See N. F. Ticehurst, *The Mute Swan in England, its History and the Ancient Custom
of Swan Keeping,* Cleaver–Hume, London 1957.

[5] Translator's note: the English-speaking reader will, of course, be reminded of
the 'Swan of Avon'.

[6] See an article by R. P. Audras, 'Au Paon, la palme de la beauté', *Découvrir les
Animaux,* No. 151, 19 March 1973, pp. 3–4.

[7] It would seem from recent discoveries that pheasants may have existed in
Europe as long ago as the Quaternary, which, if true, would throw an entirely fresh
light on the bird's history.

CHAPTER NINE

Fish, Insects and Molluscs

AS WE descend the zoological ladder, we next meet the reptiles, who have never been represented among true domestic animals. Nevertheless, there do exist alligator farms in Florida and California where these reptiles are kept in tanks by the hundred. In the Seychelles, giant turtles live in a semi-domesticated state. In Europe, a much smaller member of the same family—the Greek tortoise—is a popular pet. Despite its name, the animal in fact originates from North Africa. In West Africa, people occasionally keep pythons close to their homes to keep down rodents.

Many species of fish feature prominently in the history of the domestication of animals. Fish have been bred by man for two distinct reasons: as a source of food (fish farming), and for ornamental purposes, mainly in aquaria.

Fish farming, or pisciculture, dates from Roman times. At about 100 B.C. the Romans began installing tanks or *piscinae* (from the Latin for fish, *piscis*) in which they kept fresh-water fish. However, they also attempted to breed sea-water fish, and Lucullus—renowned for his sumptuous feasts—is known to have kept a sea-water basin for this purpose.

The Romans are said to have been very fond of the moray, a snake-like sea fish related to the eel. The moray can be up to 3 metres long, and its yellow markings give it a frightening aspect. The Romans are said to have kept moray in tanks installed on their shores. However, some of these fish must in fact have been eels, for not only were the tanks in some instances sited a considerable way inland, but they were much too small to have held the number of fish reported if these had indeed been moray.

Be this as it may, some scaring tales were told about the supposed ferocity of the moray. According to one story, a friend of the Emperor Augustus, one Vedius Pollio, ordered some of his slaves to be thrown into a pool teeming with moray fish. Revolted by such cruelty, Augustus ordered the pool to be filled up. The authenticity of this story—let us add—has since been seriously questioned.

A less fierce creature, the pet moray belonging to Senator Cassius, used to eat out of its master's hand. Cassius had the fish adorned with pearl necklaces and even ear-rings (the question is: what on earth did he fasten them to?). When the fish died, the senator went into mourning and had the creature buried with great pomp and circumstance.

For a long time, fish farming was confined purely and simply to restocking ponds with fry. In the fourteenth century, however, a French monk, Dom Pinchom, invented the technique of fertilising fish artificially. His method was perfected by the German naturalist Jacobi in the eighteenth century: used to this day, it consists of pressing the sides of the female to induce her to lay her eggs. The same procedure is then repeated with the male, to make him shed his sperm, or milt. The eggs and milt are then mixed with a spatula. This method was first brought into large-scale use in 1765 in the Duchy of Hanover.

The species bred on fish farms fall into two categories: the *Cyprinidae,* which include the tench, the Crucian or Prussian carp, and above all the common carp. There are a number of varieties of the latter, such as the mirror carp—with its characteristic rows of bright scales, and the leather carp which, by way of contrast, has no scales at all. In the lakes which dotted the grounds of the *châteaux* of the

Renaissance, huge carp were kept.[1]

There are also trout farms, as well as salmon and char hatcheries. These establishments specialise in the main in the production of fry for stocking up fisheries. So far as the rainbow trout is concerned—a fish which has come to us from the United States—these attempts have been anything but successful: boxes of eggs of this species have been placed in European rivers in the hope of stocking them with rainbow trout, but the fish introduced in this way have simply disappeared . . . It is normal practice to restock fisheries with eel and shad. This latter species is bred particularly in the U.S.A., though in France commercial shad breeding was unsuccessful.

While on the subject of pisciculture, we must also mention the 'larvivorous' fish used to destroy the larvae of the anopheles mosquito, which is responsible for the spread of malaria. Several species of these useful creatures have been imported into areas ravaged by the disease. The Gambusia fish, in particular, has been introduced into many countries to help in the fight against malaria.

*   *   *

Other species of fish are kept in aquaria with the sole aim of giving visual pleasure. The most common of these ornamental fish is the goldfish, which is simply a variety of the common carp. The interest in this fish has come to us from the Far East: numerous mutations—such as fish with huge tail fins, and others with eyes on stalks, have been bred in China since ancient times. In Greece, the goldfish was sacred to the Goddess of Love. It figures in many stories in the *Arabian Nights*. In the seventeenth century, the fashion of keeping these fish spread first to Portugal and thence to America. The goldfish was the favourite fish of Madame de Pompadour.

The popularity of the goldfish has led to the birth of a sizeable industry: whole farms have been set up in southern Europe, especially in Italy, for the purpose of breeding goldfish. Some of these establishments have an output of more than one million fish a year.

Also from the Far East comes the fighting fish, which is notable for the length of its fins and its striking, and changing, colouring. It owes its name to the aggressive habits of the males, who fight furiously among themselves. This characteristic is exploited by the people of Thailand: during the dry season—between October and April—they organise bouts between male fighting fish. There is always a good crowd on hand to watch these contests, and the betting is so fast and furious that—so at least we are told—spectators will occasionally stake their wives and children on the outcome of a fight!

During the last century, several other species of aquarium fish were introduced into Europe, notably two relations of the fighting fish, the Gourami, introduced in 1865, and the Chinese Paradise fish (1869).

*   *   *

Among insects, there are two domesticated species of outstanding importance: the bee and the silkworm. The bee was first domesticated in the Neolithic age. A rock painting in the Valencia region of Spain features a person, shown in silhouette and surrounded by bees, in the process of removing a honeycomb from a hive. A painting discovered in Turkey and dating from 6500 B.C. appears to represent the life cycle of the bee. In Russia, too, bee-keeping is said to date from the Neolithic age.

But once again it is to the ancient Egyptians that the credit must go for perfecting this art, for they are known to have improved the technique of bee-keeping in about 2600 B.C. A study of *bas-reliefs* and paintings reflects the progress of apiculture in Egypt. The Egyptians would first smoke the bees out of the hives which, incidentally, were of very simple construction, to remove the honey. Then they apparently induced the bees to return to the hive by means of decoys: that this was the procedure employed seems to be indicated by a painting of King Neuserre's Sun temple at Abu Gurab which dates from 2400 B.C., i.e. the Old Empire. The use of honey became widespread during the Middle Empire, as shown by the discovery of cakes and pots of honey dating from that period.

During the New Empire the hives were improved, as can be seen from paintings dating from about 1500 B.C.: the hives were cylindrical, made of reeds and covered with dried mud or cow dung, and open at either end. The technique of fumigation was reintroduced at this stage.

There is no mention in the Bible of the bee as such, but we know that the Israelites were fond of honey. The art of bee-keeping subsequently spread to Greece and Rome. Bees were kept on the slopes of Mount Hymettus, and Virgil devoted one of his *Georgics* to the bee. Mead, a beverage made of honey and water, was very popular in classical antiquity. From Greece, the art of bee-keeping was introduced into Babylonia at the time of the Emperor Constantine. Honey was used in the magical rites of that region.

Honey has also played an important part in the Islamic countries. In Africa, apiculture is widely practised side by side with the gathering of honey from wild bees. The American Indians kept bees long before the Spanish conquest, and honey was widely traded in Mexico.

Many scholars have taken a passionate interest in the habits of the bee, and in the eighteenth century a Dutchman, Swammerdam, undertook the first truly scientific study of the bee, while that great scientist, Réaumur, produced a rough outline of the industrious insect's biology. Some little time later, François Huber, of Geneva, although blind, published his remarkable observations of life in the beehive. In 1901 the Belgian writer Maurice Maeterlinck published his *La Vie des Abeilles*, which contains some novel concepts, notably on the social structure of the hive.

In France, the First Empire adopted the bee as its symbol, and bees were featured on the coronation robes. Less widely known is the fact that bees have, on occasion, been used as weapons of war. When King Henry I of England was besieged by the Duke of Lorraine, the commander of his garrison gave orders for bee hives to be thrown at the enemy, with the result that the encircling troops quickly took to their heels.

On another occasion, the converse procedure was employed: to conquer the citadel of Acre, which he was besieging, Richard Lionheart ordered some one hundred hives to be thrown over the walls. The defenders fled from the buzzing projectiles, abandoning the citadel to the attackers.

Royal jelly, a very nutritious substance with which bees feed their larvae, has been put to more peaceful ends: it is used as an ingredient in medicines and beauty preparations.

*   *   *

The other domesticated insect we have mentioned is the silkworm (*Bombyx mori*), whose larva—or silkworm proper—is bred for the silk it produces. This large moth with whitish wings no longer occurs in the wild state. It originates from the Far East and is probably descended from a Chinese butterfly, the species *Theophila mandarina*, with which it mates readily.

The history of the silkworm has been outlined by Jean Rostand.

We are told that it was an Empress of China, Si Ling-chi, who, about 2600 B.C., first bred silkworms. Silk production, or sericulture, had ritual and religious overtones in China and was only permitted to ladies of the nobility.

In the third century B.C. the art began to spread across Asia until it finally reached Europe. A display of it was one of the attractions at a festival held in honour of Julius Caesar in 46 B.C. Silkworm breeding also took root in India and Japan.

By the eighth century the Arabs had spread the art of silkworm breeding throughout the region bounded by Persia in the East and Spain in the West, but it was only in the thirteenth century that it was discovered in France. In 1601 the agronomist Olivier de Serres ordered some 20,000 mulberry trees to be planted in the Tuileries Gardens, and silkworm breeding continued for a long time in the Paris region, for we know that Ernesta Grisi, the friend of Théophile Gautier, practised the craft just outside Montrouge.

In the latter half of the nineteenth century sericulture went into a decline in France, but a few silkworm nurseries—which is what these establishments are called—have remained in existence to this day in the area of the River Gard. The main producer countries of natural silk are Japan, China, the U.S.S.R. and South Korea—in this order—and the most important silk marketing centres are Canton, Yokohama and Kobe.

Let us briefly describe the life cycle of the silkworm: in June the adult moth, having emerged from the cocoon, mates and lays her eggs, or 'grains', from which, in the following spring, the worms are hatched. These are, in fact, caterpillars; they are white, with dark patches. They cast their skin four times before attaining their ultimate size, which ranges from 5 to 8 cm. They feed on the leaves of the white mulberry tree; after forty days they begin to lose their appetite and crawl on to branches of the tree to spin their cocoons from the silk secreted by their salivary glands. The silk is at first viscous, but hardens on being exposed to the air. To spin a single cocoon—which can be up to 6 cm long and weigh 4 g, between 300 and 1,500 metres of silk are required. Inside the cocoon, the worm turns into a chrysalis; the latter ultimately changes into a moth.

Biologists have always been passionately interested in the silkworm, and in the seventeenth century the Italian scientist Malpighi made a study of it. In the last century a severe disease, *pebrine*, struck the silkworm nurseries. The disease is passed on by tiny unicellular creatures, *Protozoa*—in this case the *Nosema*, which belong to the sub-branch of *Sporozoa*. The spores of this parasite invade the body of the worm, which becomes infected with black spots.

The order went out to Pasteur to devise a method to combat the disease. He knew nothing about insects, however, and it was Fabre who initiated him into the secrets of the silkworm's biology. This was all the more necessary as *pebrine* is a hereditary disease: the spores enter the eggs while they are still within the body of the female and, in consequence, the larvae are infected before they are hatched. The only means of combating the disease is to separate the healthy eggs from the affected ones and to destroy the latter. Pasteur realised this and, thanks to his method, the disease was wiped out.

The mulberry silkworm is not the only source of natural silk: in India the castor plant silkworm is bred, and in Japan the oak silkworm, which produces tussor silk; this type of silk is also produced in China by a closely related species of silkworm. The Indian tussah silk is made by the larvae of the Indian moth, bred on shrubs in the open. Finally, there is the Ailanthus silkworm, which will be discussed in a later chapter.

A very different type of insect, the cochineal beetle, has been bred to produce a colouring dye; this, too, we shall discuss later.

*   *   *

Ought we to include the cricket among domesticated insects? There would seem to be a very good case for doing so. The ancient Greeks certainly kept crickets (and also grasshoppers) in cages for the pleasure of hearing them sing, and the people of the Provence used to make cages which they called '*cages à cricris*'. In China, the fashion of keeping grasshoppers in this way is very popular: people enclose the insects in all sorts of receptacles, for example in gourds which they tie to their belts. Whole books have been written in China about the care of these tiny music-makers.

Like the Indonesians and Malays, the Chinese are passionately fond of grasshopper fighting. The two adversaries are first placed in a flat dish divided by an opaque partition. They are then excited by means of a pair of fine tweezers, and the partition is raised. The two grasshoppers rush at each other; the stronger of the two will turn its opponent on its back and begin to chirp. The owner of the grasshopper that has come off worst may try to raise the loser's morale by blowing on it or picking it up by its antennae. Occasionally, the insect may be sufficiently encouraged by this treatment to resume the fight and may even turn the tables on its opponent . . . Bets are placed on the outcome of these bouts, and there have even been cases of doping: people sometimes feed the insects with red peppers. The winners' names are inscribed on ivory tablets, and when they die the grasshoppers are given an official funeral.

Another musical insect, the cicada, was much loved by the Greeks, who kept individual specimens in cages, just like the grasshoppers. Ladies would fasten cicadas to their coiffures by means of golden threads. In ancient Greece, the cicada was a symbol of music, although in fact its song is merely the rather discordant noise made by a special apparatus with which the insect is equipped, known as timbals. It is strange the Greeks should have been so fascinated by it.

One is bound to ask oneself—as did Marcel Roland—whether the Greeks did not devise a method of training the insect to produce more agreeable sounds. Yet, it may well be that they were simply fond of the creature because it is part and parcel of the Mediterranean landscape in which their civilisation was set.

Many insects, from the cockroach to the butterfly, are in fact comparatively easy to 'tame': in South America, Indian women place Corn beetles either on their clothes or in their hair. These are luminous *Coleoptera* which shine with a thousand lights. A curious fact may be worth mentioning in this context: the beetles are tied to the women's hair with fine golden chains, just as the Greek ladies used to do with their cicadas.

In conclusion, we should perhaps say a word or two about an insect which, though small in size, is of great scientific importance, for genetics, the science of heredity, greatly depends on it. We refer to *Drosophila*, or the fruit-fly, which measures 2 mm in length, and as a rule has red eyes. It feeds on ripe fruit, and to attract these insects it is enough to put out a few slices of banana on a window sill.

Drosophila is of twofold interest to the biologist: its reproductive cycle is very rapid, and countless mutations—i.e. inherited variations in the shape of the eyes, the wings, etc.—occur.

* * *

Among crustaceans, there is only one which needs to be mentioned in this context: the crayfish, which is raised in tanks where natural conditions are reproduced as closely as possible, thus creating an environment in which these creatures will breed readily. Crayfish culture is practised both in Europe and America.

Several species of spider have been bred for their silk.[2] In 1709, a Montpellier official displayed before the Academy in that city gloves and stockings made of spider silk . . . Louis XIV ordered Réaumur to investigate the matter, and in 1710 the latter published his *Examen de la soie des araignées*. In this work he suggested that exotic species should be used for this purpose. However, both in France and in Britain, clever inventors devised ways of producing spider silk from local species.

Rather than comb the countryside for spiders, it seemed more efficient to breed the creatures, and at the beginning of the nineteenth century two Frenchmen, Dubois father and son, established a nursery where they raised no fewer than 400,000 spiders! They kept common house spiders in boxes and fed them on meat and insects.

Unfortunately, the silk output of these spiders was poor and, just as Réaumur had predicted, tropical spiders had to be used. A missionary, Father Camboué, was impressed with the strength of the thread spun by the Madagascar *Nephila*: its web was capable of sustaining weights of up to 500 g. At the end of the last century, the decision was therefore taken to use this species. At first the method employed was to hold the spiders in the hand to make them release their silk. This, however, did not prove very efficient and it was decided to enclose the creatures in boxes from which their abdomen protruded, so that the silk could be collected as it was released. A single *Nephila* produced nearly 4,000 metres of silk thread a month. At the 1900 World Exhibition in Paris, a canopy for a four-poster bed made of spider silk was shown.

People again returned to the idea of setting up spider nurseries, but the attempt failed. In fact, the capture of excessive numbers of *Nephila* spiders led to a proliferation of insects and a recrudescence of malaria. The experiment was therefore abandoned. Perhaps we should mention in passing that in the Solomon Islands in the Pacific, the silk of *Nephila* spiders is used for making small fishing nets.

*   *   *

Among molluscs there are several important domesticated species, though it would perhaps be more accurate in this case to speak of farming rather than domestication.

In North Africa, snails were eaten as long ago as the Neolithic age, but it was the Romans who were the first to set up snail nurseries in special enclosures known as *cochlearia*. These were as a rule sited on islands to make sure the snails could not escape. To maintain the desired degree of humidity, the creatures were kept close to the mouth of a water pipe. They were fed on a little bran and laurel leaves. The breeding of the large Burgundy snail was for a long time concentrated in that region: about the end of the nineteenth century there were numerous *escargotières* in Burgundy, and a single one of these, near Dijon, averaged some 100,000 snails a year. During the Second World War, prisoners of war were made to look after snail nurseries in Hungary.

Two other types of molluscs—marine ones in this case—command an even wider following in our own day and age. As you have probably guessed, we refer to the mussels and oysters.

Mussel breeding is said to date from the thirteenth century, although its exact beginnings are hidden in the mists of time. At about 1235, a boat with three Irishmen on board is said to have been wrecked in the Bay of Aiguillon, in the Vendée region of France. There was only one survivor, Patrick Walton, the skipper. He settled down in the area and, to survive, tried to catch sea birds by means of nets strung between posts. Walton noticed that these nets were soon covered with mussels. The shipwrecked sailor thereupon persuaded the local people to put down hundreds of stakes in the bay and planted quantities of young mussels close by. This was the beginning of systematic mussel farming, although mussels have in fact been prized by gourmets since antiquity. In our own day there are mussel nurseries along the coast of Brittany, in the Charente-Maritime Department and in the Languedoc region.

Oyster culture is older than the mussel industry. It was practised in the far distant past both by the Chinese and the Romans, who were extremely fond of oysters. The Chinese use bamboo sticks, to which the larvae of the oyster attach themselves. About 200 B.C. a Roman named Sergius Orata established oyster beds in a lake which has since silted up.

For a long time, the oyster industry made little headway, for the exploitation of natural oyster beds sufficed to meet the demand. It was only in the nineteenth century that oyster culture really began to expand. Until that time, the only species cultivated was the flat oyster. Towards 1860, this species was becoming rare and so the French producers decided to import Portuguese oysters. They planted them in a bay not far from Bordeaux, the Bassin d'Arcachon. The shell of this species has valves of unequal size.

In 1868, the good ship *Morlaisien*, with a cargo of these oysters on board, was caught in a storm and ran for shelter in the Gironde estuary, where the skipper decided to dump the cargo into the sea. The oysters prospered in this environment and multiplied to such an extent that by 1907 they covered the entire coast from the Vendée to the Gironde rivers. At the present time the main French oyster breeding grounds are those of Brittany (Cancale, Paimpol, Auray, Le Croisic, etc.) and those of the Atlantic Coast further south (Les Sables d'Olonne, Marennes, the island of Oléron, Arcachon, etc.). While in Brittany only flat oysters are produced, both species are bred further south.

Other molluscs are valued for their pearls, and the *Aviculidae* and *Meleagrina*—wrongly called pearl oysters—are in fact bred expressly for this purpose. This is how pearls are produced: when a parasite or a grain of sand happens to enter the body of the mollusc, the latter surrounds it with a layer of nacre. To encourage this process, the Chinese used to place tin figurines within the shells of fresh water mussels, thus ensuring that they were covered with a layer of nacre. Towards 1920 a Japanese, Mikimoto, invented a more efficient method: a small ball of glass or some other substance is grafted into the body of a *Meleagrina* oyster and thus made into a pearl. Based on the use of this technique, entire pearl oyster farms have been set up in Japan.

Some considerable time ago people also used to breed leeches. This segmented worm was used as a remedy against cerebral congestion and apothecaries therefore stocked leeches in their shops in special jars. The creature was placed behind a patient's ear to 'bleed' him. The method was anything but hygienic and is no longer in use.

About 1862, people first began to grow sponges, first in the Adriatic and later in Florida and Tunisia. The technique used was to place pieces of sponge on supports so as to make each piece grow into an entire new sponge. However, the industry proved unprofitable and was therefore abandoned.

[1] In recent times, a new use has been found for carp: they help to clear overgrown lakes and ponds of algae.

[2] See an article by R. Tercafs, 'Des gants d'araignée', *Découvrir les Animaux*, No. 1, 26 February 1973, p. 4.

CHAPTER TEN

Forgotten Domestications

THE SPONGE is not the first case we have mentioned of an abandoned attempt at domesticating a living creature. Let us recall, for example, the small carnivores once used to keep down rodents but now displaced by the cat, and also the case of the African elephant. There are many other such instances, and it might be interesting to review them briefly. Occasionally it is difficult to make a clear distinction between fact and legend, and there are conflicting accounts of a number of processes of domestication.

One example is that of the Giant Patagonian sloth, which has given rise to a good deal of controversy. While the extant South American varieties of the sloth are of modest size, they had giant forebears in the Quaternary era; one of them, the *Megatherium*, was the size of an elephant. Another variety—rather smaller but as big as an ox nevertheless—survived until comparatively recent times in Patagonia, where the Indians knew it well. This animal has had a number of scientific names, notably *Mylodon* and *Glossotherium*. It resembled a large, shaggy bear with powerful claws. Its skin was reinforced with a shield of interwoven ossicles, and the animal probably spent much of its time sitting on its hind quarters.

We mention the *Mylodon* because there is evidence that it may have been domesticated, or at least kept in captivity, by the Indians. In 1895, in a huge cave in Patagonia, as large as a cathedral, there was found in addition to the remains of several giant sloths, a heap of dry straw and dung. The entrance to the cave was almost wholly closed off by a wall of rubble, and there were indications that *Mylodons* were held captive in this cave. The Indians may have driven the animals into these caves and kept them there until such time as they decided to slaughter them for food.

America was also the scene of another such mystery. We know that in the Tertiary and Quaternary, varieties of the elephant which differed widely in appearance, the *Mastodons*, inhabited a large part of the world—even the Andean *Cordillera*, which is rather extraordinary since there are few large mountain animals.

There is evidence which suggests that some of the *Mastodons* may have survived beyond the dawn of history and that they were domesticated by the Mayas. A pillar found in Honduras on which 'elephants' are depicted with mahouts on their backs would appear to indicate this. The evidence is, however, too meagre to be considered conclusive.

*   *   *

The Sumerians, who in Mesopotamia established one of the oldest civilisations on record, used the onager as a draught animal. Nowadays, the onager is a very rare wild ass, having been supplanted as a domestic animal by the horse. It has been claimed that Christ rode on an onager when he entered Jerusalem on Palm Sunday.

As we have noted repeatedly, the ancient Egyptians were past masters of the art of domestication and experimented with a large range of species. We know this thanks to the *bas-reliefs* and paintings featuring animals in situations which allow no doubt that these creatures must have been at least partially domesticated.

This applies, from 4000 B.C. onward, to various species of the antelope—the *Bubalis*, *Oryx*, *Addax*, etc. These creatures were kept overnight in stables and put out to pasture during the day.[1] The same may be true of the wild goat.

A painted chest which forms part of the Tutankhamun treasure depicts a man holding a dozen dogs by a lead, and among them one can recognise a hyena. The Egyptians undoubtedly used hyenas, as well as leopards, jackals and even the lycaon (or African painted dog), for hunting. Hedgehogs were used by the Egyptians to keep down reptiles.

Pelicans, Egyptian geese, laughing geese, as well as cranes—and notably the Numidian crane—were all domesticated by the Egyptians to a greater or lesser degree. The last of these birds seems to have been used to guard farmyard poultry. The Egyptians also bred the Hamadryas monkey of the *Cynbocephalus* family, chiefly for ritual purposes.

They also kept semi-domesticated lions, and the Pharaohs Amenhotep II and Rameses the Great used these beasts in battle. The tradition of keeping tame lions lived on for a long time in the Middle East, and there was a time when it was by no means unusual to see these animals stretched out in doorways of palaces in Persia and Turkey. It is, of course, well known that the Emperor of Ethiopia kept tame lions.

A splendid Mediterranean marsh bird, the Sultan hen, was very popular among various peoples of antiquity. This is a large moorhen with blue plumage and a red beak and feet. It is said to have been regarded as sacred by the ancient Libyans and is known to have been kept as a domestic bird by the Greeks and Romans. Because of its splendid plumage, this fine species can still be seen in parks.

The Romans also bred quail, but were afraid to eat them because they thought them poisonous. On the other hand, they considered the dormouse a delicacy and raised these attractive rodents in special enclosures called *gliraria* (from the Latin *glis*—dormouse). This was, of course, the true dormouse and not the garden dormouse; our country folk are apt to confuse the two. These enclosures were surrounded by smooth walls to prevent the animals from escaping. The Romans planted oaks in their *gliraria* to provide acorns for the inmates. Nesting boxes were also put out for them.

Occasionally the Romans would fatten these rodents. They placed them in earthenware vessels, about 1 metre high, covered with a lid. Inside there was a spiral ramp to enable the animals to move about. There were holes in these jars to admit air and a glimmer of light. The tiny captives were fed on acorns, nuts and chestnuts. Such vessels were found at Pompeii. In the opening chapter of *Salammbô*, Flaubert describes a feast at which the guests were treated to 'dormouse pickled in honey'.

*   *   *

It seems that in antiquity certain peoples succeeded, if not in domesticating at least in harnessing the red deer. The Goths harnessed these animals to the carriages of 'Very Important Persons'. On Mont Gravet, in the Champagne region, the skeleton of a deer has been found dating from the time of the ancient Gauls, with a piece of the harness—the bit—placed beneath the skull. In China, during the reign of the Chou Dynasty, which ruled from 1112 to 255 B.C., the red deer, too, is said to have been more or less domesticated. Finally, according to Hue Shan, the Chinese explorer whom we have mentioned before, the American Indians, in the fifth century A.D., bred fallow deer in order to make an alcoholic beverage from the fermented milk of the female.

Various people have repeatedly tried to domesticate another animal—the zebra—but so far without great success. It would help if this animal could be domesticated since it is resistant to the *trypanosome* parasite which, in Africa, is transmitted by the dreaded tsetse-fly. Provided it is captured while still young, the zebra will submit to being either harnessed or ridden. The Romans used to do this to display animals of the species we now call Grévy's zebra—whose natural habitat is Ethiopia and the nearby territories—in their circuses. The species is called after President Grévy of France, to whom the Negus of Ethiopia presented a specimen in 1882. More recently, Hagenbeck, the director of the Hamburg zoo, succeeded in training a number of Grévy's zebras for circus work. The zebra will mate readily with a horse or a donkey, and the hybrids are easy to tame. Few people now remember that at the beginning of this century zebrulas (zebra × horse crosses) were used as draught animals in Paris, while in South Africa the true quagga—a variety of zebra now extinct—has also been used as a draught animal.

According to the film producer and ethnographer J. Rouch, the Sorko people of the Middle Niger used to raise hippopotami in a state of semi-freedom. The Dinka people of the Upper Nile are said to have succeeded in taming the giraffe, while it is reported that the

Incas bred the vicuna for its wool. Another success in the art of
domestication which is now a matter of past history takes us back to
Europe, to be more exact to the French Court. The ladies of the
Court of Charles IX are said to have kept corsacs—a fox from
southern Asia—instead of dogs.

While no one will ever again see a zebrula or a corsac in Paris, one
does occasionally glimpse a surprising sight: a large moth, almost the
size of a bat—the Ailanthus moth. In 1856, this species, with greenish
wings and white markings, was introduced into Europe from China
because its larvae produce silk. Its commercial use was subsequently
abandoned, and the moth regained its freedom. It has since become
well established in Europe's urban centres, anywhere near an
ailanthus shrub or a Japan varnish tree—plants which are fairly
common in Paris and other cities.

[1] On the tomb of Sabon (beginning of the Fifth Dynasty) it is stated that the dead
man was the owner of 5,378 head of cattle, 1,308 oryx, 1,244 addax, and 1,135
gazelles.

CHAPTER ELEVEN

The Process and the Effects of Domestication

WE HAVE now come to the end of the list of species man has attempted, with varying degrees of success, to domesticate during the course of history. As we descended the scale of living beings, from the dog to the oyster, we noted the gradual lessening of the psychological symbiosis between man and the various domestic animals concerned.

Domestication occurs in many shapes and forms, according to the species of animal involved. The variety is in fact so great that it is difficult to provide an exact definition of the term 'domestication'.

Its etymology, incidentally, does not help us very much: the word is derived from the Latin *domus*, which means house. However, the epithet 'domestic' is applied equally to animals which live *upon* houses, such as sparrows, and to those which live *in* houses, such as flies. And yet these species must be considered wild, albeit that they live in close proximity to man.

The domestic animals we are interested in are those utilised by man for whatever reason. It would be wrong, however, to regard all these animals as subservient to man. Take the cat, for instance and, to a lesser extent, the dog: both have lost whatever utilitarian function they may once have fulfilled to become pets. In this respect they come into the same category as the hamster, the guinea-pig, cage birds, etc.

A distinction must be made between domestication on the one hand and the taming and training of animals on the other. One can keep a tame crow or fennec in one's house, but it would be wrong to regard these creatures as domesticated in the true sense of the word. The same applies to circus animals. Yet, the training of an animal for a utilitarian purpose can turn into a sort of domestication: thus, a mongoose trained to kill snakes can, at a pinch, be considered a domestic animal.

Another important factor is the control man exercises over the reproduction of animals. Some experts believe that species which reproduce themselves free from human control cannot be considered domesticated. Such a view seems to us to go too far, for it would exclude, for example, the elephant, whose importance in human history has been so great, and even the alley cat which, as its master knows only too well, reproduces its kind at random.

Another criterion which is frequently applied is that of the modification of the outward aspect of a species. Those species over which man has the most control have changed to a very considerable degree as a result of selection, which has imparted to the different races and breeds great variety in terms of size and colour. Suffice it to mention in this connection the cat, the dog, as well as the various breeds of cattle, the horse, the domestic fowl, the pigeon, etc. And yet, not to regard as domesticated those species which do not exhibit such a degree of 'polymorphism'—for instance, the buffalo, the camel, the donkey and the guinea-fowl—would also be wide of the mark.

The methods used by man to master animals vary unduly. It hardly needs saying that the methods used in domesticating mammals will not do for molluscs. However, regardless of the animal involved, the general nature of the process does not vary much.

To begin with, man isolates a small number of specimens from their fellows, thus preventing them from mating indiscriminately. Before long, this first domesticated animal population—whose reproduction takes place within a closed group—is sufficiently large to make it unnecessary for the breeder to capture additional specimens.

This state of sexual isolation is of capital importance in the process of domestication, for once a species has come under man's control, he can pass on to the second stage of the process, that of artificial selection. By judicious crossing of domesticated animals, he improves their characteristics: it is thus that race horses become faster and faster, and hens lay more and more eggs.

This last example is particularly striking. In 1925, a hen which laid 112 eggs a year was considered a good layer; nowadays the 'output' of a laying bird is about 220 eggs, while the record is no less than 361 eggs, i.e. nearly an egg a day! At the same time, poultry have also gained in terms of weight. Efficient selection consists in improving average performance rather than in producing individual 'prize' specimens.

The aim of artificial selection is to stabilise the desirable mutations of a species. As the reader may know, a mutation is a variation due to a genetic 'accident' at the chromosome level—chromosomes are minute rods in the nuclei of cells—capable of being passed on from generation to generation. It is thus that the first basset hound came into being, the first sailfin goldfish, the first naked-necked fowl, etc. In nature, such mutations stand little chance of perpetuating themselves. In effect, a 'mutant'—being as a rule unique of its kind—is of necessity bound to mate with a normal specimen, and the qualities characteristic of the mutation are usually 'dominated' by the normal characteristics. The qualities of the mutant are therefore called 'recessive'—which is to say that they are liable to disappear very quickly.

The situation is quite different where domesticated animals are concerned. Man can see to it that identical mutants will mate, with the result that their characteristics are passed on to their offspring.

*   *   *

Over the centuries, under the impact of domestication and selection, the appearance of a considerable number of species has thus changed significantly. This is why—as we have noted—it is difficult to establish the identity of the wild ancestors of certain animals—since most of their original characteristics have by now been bred out of them.

These changes take place step by step and thus provide useful guidance to archaeologists and palaeontologists. The transformation is in fact so gradual that it is often quite difficult to determine if the remains of an individual animal are those of a domesticated or of a wild specimen.

Yet, there are a number of indicators which can help the scientist in this regard. Thus, tooth decay is usually a mark of domestication since the food given to domestic animals, because of its lack of variety, is apt to cause caries. Where an animal is forced to carry loads, this leads to changes in the joints and toe bones. A very marked characteristic distinguishes the skull of a dog from that of the wolf: in the wolf, the length of each of the upper canine teeth is greater than that of the two molars put together, which is not the case with the dog.

As a rule, domestication leads to a reduction in the size of the animal concerned. From the stone age onwards, the cattle in Denmark had smaller lower molars than the aurochs, and their carpal bones were also smaller. In Palestine, pigs exhibited a similar symptom: their skulls were at first comparatively small due to arrested growth rather than because of the presence of specimens small from birth; later however, farmers undoubtedly deliberately sought to select small animals to breed from because their offspring were easier to manage.

The mouths, horns and tails of domesticated breeds also tend, with time, to diminish in size. The famous Manx cats are the most striking example of such a shrinkage of the extremities. The wild Chinese goose has an elongated beak and a backward sloping forehead: the domesticated variety has a knob above the beak and a pouch under the throat. Lack of exercise, a sedentary existence and the availability of an abundance of food often lead to obesity. Also the musculature, and above all the jaws, of domesticated breeds tend to diminish in size. On the other hand, as a result of selection, a domesticated variety may acquire a specialised muscle structure: the racehorse is a case in point.

Domestication also affects the colour of an animal's coat or plumage. As we have seen from many examples, the colouring of domesticated breeds tends to be much more varied than that of their wild ancestors. Piebald—i.e. black and white—colouring is frequently encountered among domesticated animals, for example, cattle, horses and dogs, while it is rare among wild species, since these conspicuous colours make it difficult for a wild animal to merge into the background. Yet, it is a fact that some wild animals with this sort of colouring thrive just the same, such as the magpie, from whose name the word 'piebald' is in fact derived.

A domestic existence also invariably results in physiological and psychological changes. The most important of these concerns the reproductive cycle: unlike their wild ancestors, domestic animals mate more or less at all times of the year and not at set seasons. Moreover, they are able to produce offspring at an earlier age: a dog, for example, can produce a litter at one year old, while the corresponding age for a wolf is two years.

The nervous system is also affected: the brain of domestic animals tends to be about twenty per cent lighter than that of the most closely related wild species. This 'decadence' affects the animals' mental powers: the tame rabbit is far less intelligent than the wild variety, and compared with the sewer rat the white rat must be considered a degenerate breed which has lost most of the faculties of its wild counterpart.

Lorenz has studied the domestic goose in this regard: its behaviour pattern shows obvious signs of a psychological decline: the gander does not mark out his territory (the area around the nest which birds protect against intruders), he neglects his paternal duties and will court any female in sight—though some might be tempted to ask whether this can really be regarded as a symptom of decadence . . .! Be that as it may, the domestic goose is polygamous while its wild ancestor was monogamous.

It would be wrong, however, to regard this degeneration as universal: dogs and cats are highly intelligent and subtle—more so, perhaps, than their wild ancestors. Yet, the mental make-up of the domestic dog and cat has undoubtedly changed in some respects. So far as the dog is concerned, the various parts of the brain have become smaller in relation to the volume of information transmitted by the corresponding sensory organs.

In fact, domestication results in a transformation of an animal's nervous and endocrinal systems. This view is borne out by the work of the Russian biologist D. K. Belyaev, Director of the Institute of Cytology and Genetics at Akademgorodok (Sverdlovsk) of the U.S.S.R. Academy of Sciences. He breeds silver foxes in Siberia and has found that some specimens are remarkably docile, resembling dogs in that respect. The interesting thing is that these foxes breed at an earlier age than aggressive specimens and that they are also more fertile. In other words, they have progressed further along the road to domestication and their character has been modified by their masters.

CHAPTER TWELVE

From the Cave to the Apartment Block

THROUGHOUT HISTORY, and even in pre-historic times, man has lived side by side with animals he has succeeded in taming, and they have played an important part in his life.

Let us recall, for example, that there are civilisations based on the reindeer and the llama, and let us remember, too, the part played by the cat in ancient Egypt. Domesticated and, for that matter, wild animals as well, have always loomed large in man's religious observances, in his customs, beliefs and legends.

In prehistoric times, man's closest companions in his caves and lake settlements were, above all, the dog, the goat and the sheep. The domestication of these animals marked an important stage in the evolution of humanity, when man passed from a 'predatory' economy—based on hunting, fishing and the gathering of berries, etc.—to an economy relying on production, i.e. agriculture and animal husbandry. This is what is meant by the expression 'neolithic revolution'.

It is worth noting in this context that there was no pastoral life in America prior to the European conquest. Yet, the American Indians belong to a yellow-skinned race from Asia whose peoples at one time practised the pastoral way of life. The fact is that the New World was devoid of animals suitable for domestication.

*   *   *

In some regions, men and animals have at times lived in close proximity. This used to be true, for instance, of certain parts of France, where the same door served both the domestic animals and their owners, and all that separated masters from livestock was a wicker partition. In the Languedoc, the stables also served as entrance hall.

In the Aveyron region, cattle and pigs lived on the ground floor, while the first floor was shared by the family and their poultry, including geese and piglets. The children crawled on the floor amidst a welter of animals.

In the Hautes-Alpes this mixed way of life was taken even further: to face up to the rigours of the Alpine winter, beasts and humans huddled together for months on end in the same room, which normally contained three or four beds where goats and sheep slept side by side with members of the family. The pigs kept to the corners of this remarkable bedroom; the horses, cows and oxen occupied the rest of the space along the walls, while the middle was reserved for the calves. For six months on end, the dung would be allowed to pile up and was not removed until after Easter! The atmosphere in the room does not bear thinking of. Such habits may perhaps still be found in some parts of France, nor is it unknown for a farmer's wife to offer her bed and the warmth of her eiderdowns to a brood of chicks or ducklings. Once they have grown a little, the birds are allowed to pick crumbs off the table.

The result of all this was that the animals became part and parcel of the family. In Normandy, for example, people used to adorn their animals with tufts of red wool; on the death of a member of the family, these were replaced with blue wool. Among Walloon country folk it used to be the custom for farmers to wish their animals a happy new year.

Such examples are not confined to Europe. In the Kabyl region of Algeria, for example, the one and only room of the traditional house was partitioned by a low wall: the people lived on one side and their horses and cattle on the other. In Annam, only a few planks in one corner of the house separated the family buffalo from its owners. Finally, in the Tonkin region of Indochina, it is still customary for buffaloes, pigs and poultry to sleep in the space between the pillars which support the village houses.

*   *   *

In our own day, a new companionship has evolved between animals on the one hand and their owners on the other. Prisoner in a world of concrete and asphalt in the cities of Europe, where greenery is all too rare a sight, the townsman tends more and more to look to animals for company. To him, a cat, a dog or, at worst, a canary or a tortoise provide a glimpse of nature.

The importance which pets play in the life of French city folk is reflected in the following figures: there are at present some nine million cats in France (which is a European record), as well as 6,500,000 dogs. Western France alone accounts for one-quarter of the dogs and one-fifth of the cats in the country. In the villages, there are on average 236 dogs per 1,000 of the population, compared with forty in the cities. There has been a rapid rise in these figures: in 1783 there were only 1,800,000 dogs in France as against 2,900,000 in 1897 and more than three million in 1900.

Twenty-nine per cent of all French homes have at least one dog, compared with 45 per cent in Ireland and a mere 27 per cent in Britain; 25 per cent in Denmark; Belgium 22 per cent; Italy 19 per cent and Germany 9 per cent. In France, these figures vary from region to region: in Paris the proportion of homes where dogs are kept is as low as 10 per cent, compared with 50 per cent in western and south-western France. For cats, the figures are as follows: Ireland 38 per cent; Portugal 28 per cent; Finland 28 per cent; France 25 per cent; Italy 23 per cent; Belgium 21 per cent; Britain 12 per cent and Germany 9 per cent.[1] Finally, cage birds are found in 14 per cent of all French homes, compared with 23 per cent in Belgium; 21 per cent in the Netherlands; Britain 14 per cent; Germany 13 per cent; Spain 12 per cent and Finland 1 per cent.

Single people are particularly fond of cats and dogs: in France 452,000 single persons own a dog and 588,000 a cat. The presence of children tends to encourage the acquisition of a pet, and the same applies, of course, where a family owns a garden. Various types of social, professional, or even family and matrimonial, frustrations may lead to the purchase of a cat or a dog: there is here a fruitful area for the sociologist to research.

Dog ownership is now becoming more and more popular in working-class districts. This is true, above all, of certain large breeds such as the Alsatian and, in France, the Beauceron breed. The owners of such animals belong to breed clubs and societies, where they spend much of their free time: such clubs have become especially numerous in the eastern suburbs of Paris.

We have mentioned figures relating to cage birds: their total number in France is about six million, owned by three million people. In Britain, the number of owners has been estimated at six million; in the United States between twenty and thrity million birds are owned by ten million people. As for budgeriagars and parrots, there are said to be more than five million in Britain compared with a mere fifteen thousand in France. This latter total is as small as this because of the measures that are being enforced to combat psittacosis.

*   *   *

The rapid rise in the number of pets kept in an urban environment has resulted in the emergence of new problems. First of all, the diverse activities linked with pet ownership (pet shops, kennels, etc.) have so far been allowed to flourish unchecked by any attempt at co-ordination. Modern town planning ought to allow for this new companionship of man and animal. For instance, any newly built apartment blocks should be equipped with an 'animal day nursery'. The problem posed by the fouling of pavements and footpaths should be tackled by setting aside areas reserved for owners and their pets. Incidentally, dog urinals have recently been installed in a number of towns—Nice, for example.

'Animal day nurseries' are particularly desirable in the more remote suburbs, where dog owners, who for the most part work in the city centre, are forced to leave their pets alone for most of the day. Such 'crèches' would solve the problem of the dogs' loneliness. Dog and cat owners have to contend with a great many prohibitions when travelling with their pets by rail or underground, or when they want to take their pet with them to a hotel. Special facilities should be made available to people who wish to travel without having to be separated from their pets.

There is much to be said for schools keeping animals: a budding naturalist will show signs of this interest at a very early age; if he or she is enabled to observe animals at close quarters, this is bound to be helpful. It is an excellent idea for young people to raise small pets such as hamsters, guinea-pigs or white mice and will, incidentally, teach them the facts of life. On the other hand, very young children should not be allowed to own animals, for youngsters are apt to be deeply upset by the death of a pet; older children come to terms more easily with the disappearance of a beloved companion.

The presence of ornamental animals, such as swans and deer, is coming to be valued more and more as a means of helping the towns-man find relief from the tensions of urban life.

The proximity of domestic animals is so beneficial to man that pets are in fact being used for certain types of medical treatment. Dogs, for instance, can help problem children adjust to their environment; this 'cynotherapy' has produced some very promising results.

The company of ponies has proved helpful in the training of mentally retarded children, and for some time now it has been customary to take children suffering from psychological disorders on regular visits to pony clubs. At Sèvres, near Paris, an institution which specialises in treating such children is working in close liaison with the local pony club.

The fact that ponies and children are of roughly equal size helps a lot. The child is able to feel superior to the pony, both physically and intellectually, since the pony obeys his orders. This enables the child gradually to acquire self-confidence; his command of language improves, and the word 'pony' is sometimes the first he learns to pronounce. We know of a case of a young boy who for two years refused to get on a pony and would do so only when it was made clear to him that he would not be allowed to join the rest of his class, who were about to leave for a spell in the country. Once he had made friends with ponies, he managed to rid himself of his habit of bed-wetting.

Alas, the animals themselves sometimes suffer psychological damage because of the very fact that they have been made into an object of fashion. For example, breeders, to satisfy a passing whim of the public, will go in for intensive hybridisation without regard to the need to avoid inbreeding. As a result, 'problem dogs' are produced—nervous, unstable and aggressive animals. The dalmatians are a notable case in point. Dogs bred primarily for showing tend to lack stamina and resistance to disease. Life in kennels is frequently fatal to puppies, whose health is undermined by the isolation in which they are kept.

[1] Although France is not the leading country in Europe in terms of the percentage of cat owners, the total cat population is the largest of any country in Europe, and many homes, in fact, have more than one cat.

CHAPTER THIRTEEN

The Other Side of the Coin

THE DOMESTICATION of animals has its less attractive side. Animals that man ought to have treated as his friends have in fact been subjected to the most odious tortures—we have already cited the example of the cat—and have sometimes been put to death after a mock trial. For countless centuries, animals were hanged, burnt alive, beaten to death, strangled and then burnt and their remains scattered to the winds . . .

We know a good deal about these mediaeval animal trials, for two writers, Michel Rousseau and Jean Vartier, have published a number of fascinating accounts on this subject. These practices may well have had their origin in a passage in the Bible (Exodus, XXI, 28–32), which says:

> If an ox gore a man or woman, that they die: then the ox shall be surely stoned, and his flesh shall not be eaten, but the owner of the ox shall be quit. But if the

ox were wont to push with his horn in time past and it hath been testified to his owner and he hath not kept him in, but that he hath killed a man or a woman; the ox shall be stoned and his owner also shall be put to death.

If there be laid on him a sum of money, then he shall give, for the ransom of his life whatsoever is laid on him. Whether he have gored a son or have gored a daughter, according to this judgment shall it be done unto him. If the ox push a man-servant or a maid-servant; he shall give unto their master thirty shekels of silver and the ox shall be stoned.

The chief victim of these animal trials was the pig. As we have noted, these animals were allowed to roam the streets freely and accidents inevitably occurred. A document dating from this time tells of the execution of a sow at Fontenay-aux-Roses, just outside Paris:

In the year of grace 1348, or thereabouts, a pig was apprehended at Fontenay after it had eaten a child, one Etienne le Camus, and the pig was burnt in the courtyard of the town hall of the said place.

A fresco in the Church of the Holy Trinity at Falaise in the Calvados Department depicts the execution, in 1386, of a sow which had been sentenced to death on charges of having killed a child. To make it look more like a human being, the beast was dressed up in a jacket; white gloves were put on its forefeet and a pair of breeches on the hind quarters. The sow was hanged before a large crowd.

In 1405, a bull was hanged at Gisors. In 1463, in Amiens, a watchman received payment for 'having buried two pigs which had gashed and bitten a small child, as a result of which the latter departed this life'.

In 1474, a cock was burnt alive in Basle for having—believe it or not—laid an egg! . . . and in 1557 a piglet was buried alive at Saint-Quentin for having eaten a child. The same sort of thing happened in the Vosges mountains in 1572. The reading of the sentence of death was preceded and followed by a solemn roll of drums. In fact, it was the customs of the time, which allowed pigs to roam at will, rather than the animals themselves, which were responsible for these accidents. Occasionally—this is known to have happened at Saint-Omer, for instance—the carcass of a pig that had been hanged would be left dangling from the gallows for years on end . . .[1]

In the seventeenth century, these animal trials found an echo in Racine's comedy *Les Plaideurs*, in which a dog is made to appear before a court of law. As late as the eighteenth century pigs and goats caught damaging vineyards were liable to be killed by the growers.

*   *   *

Such trials are more readily understood if one bears in mind that in the eyes of the people of that time animals were closely linked with magic and sorcery. Its folklore and literature therefore abound with stories of human beings who had been transformed into animals. Ovid's *Metamorphoses* are a case in point. Later, it was the wolf which tended to be the central figure of such beliefs. The werewolf—a man changed into a wolf which roams the countryside by night—is the subject of one such myth. According to other folk tales human beings change into cats. One such story is told by Claude Seignolle in his *Contes fantastiques de Bretagne*.[2]

A peasant called Croxanvic one night picked up beside a crucifix a big, long-haired cat. He took it home with him but then made no attempt to look after it. On the contrary, he kicked and beat it all day long. Yet, the cat did not try to run away in spite of the vile treatment to which it was being subjected. And then a strange transformation occurred: Croxanvic all of a sudden felt an urge to hunt for mice and began to be able to see in the dark. He would arch his back at the sight of a dog and lap up his soup with his tongue. In short, he had turned into a cat.

The real cat had now become a rival to him and so he decided to kill it. One day he lured the cat beneath a heavy crucible and poured the molten metal it contained over it. Some time later, Croxanvic was found lying on his back in a field, his eyes turned up and his tongue hanging out . . . When the owner of the crucible turned it the right way up, he found nothing underneath.

*   *   *

In many civilisations animals were sacrificed in the course of religious rites. The Hebrews observed three types of sacrificial ceremonies: the holocaust (when the victims were burnt alive), sacrifices which went hand in hand with prayer, and sacrifices of thanksgiving. In each case, the animals were put to death in a temple. There was only one exception to this rule: the scapegoat. On the Day of Atonement, the High Priest would solemnly curse the animal and place the burden of blame for all the sins of the Jews upon it. The goat was then chased into the desert to be devoured by wild beasts.

In India and China horses and goats were used in sacrificial rites. The Greeks would drown animals as a sacrifice to the water gods, while they buried in the earth the blood of beasts they had sacrificed to the gods of the underworld. Sheep and cattle were sacrificed in Delphi to entreat the goddess to vouchsafe her oracles.

In Rome, it was the pig which was the main victim of official and religious ceremonial. Each time a contract was signed a pig would be put to death. To mark the signing of an international treaty, the representatives of Rome and the foreign power concerned would go to the Temple of Jupiter, where the priest pronounced the following formula: 'If the Roman people break this treaty, may Jupiter strike them as I am about to strike this pig.' He then killed a sacrificial pig with a sacred knife.

White oxen were sacrificed to Jupiter and Juno, while the Goddess Ceres was entitled to the sacrifice of a ewe in lamb, the symbol of fertility. At the beginning of the Second Punic War, the Roman Senate ordered a 'sacred spring' to be observed, which meant that countless animals born that spring were put to death.

Each year, at the beginning of February male goats and dogs would be sacrificed to mark the feast of the *Lupercalia*. The priests performing this ceremonial were dressed in goat skins. They ran a race during which they whipped women wishing to be cured of sterility with thongs made of their animal victims' hides. And while we are on the subject of Roman rites, let us remind the reader of the sanguinary ceremony of the *Taurobolus*.

*   *   *

As we have repeated again and again, man has throughout history taken an evil pleasure in forcing animals to fight one another. The ancient Romans organised bouts between all sorts of animals in their circuses, though more often wild beasts were involved rather than domestic animals.

As recently as the last century dogfights were still common. In France, this custom did not disappear until 1834. Just as cruel a sport involved rats and dogs. These contests were held in a pit surrounded on all sides with mirrors. The ringmaster, who always wore tights and soft leather boots, first set a ratter dog on to a rat and then, one by one, released four more rats into the pit. A panel of judges, watch in hand, timed how long it took each dog to kill a set of five rats. The dog which took the least time was the winner. Some ratter dogs took as little as thirty seconds to accomplish this feat. The last of these revolting spectacles was held in the Champs-Elysées as recently as June 1870.

*   *   *

One of the drawbacks of domestication is that the animals are liable to infect those who look after them. Thus, *anthrax*, a disease which once upon a time used to decimate sheep, cattle, pigs, horses, goats, etc., was liable to be transmitted to anyone who handled products made from these animals, such as wool and hides. The disease causes boils and swellings.

For a long time, the origin of the disease remained a mystery. However, in 1850, a French bacteriologist, C. J. Davaine, discovered in the blood of sheep affected by anthrax minute rod-shaped organisms. These were the bacteria which caused the disease.

At that stage, this hypothesis still remained to be proven, but in 1876 a German physician, Robert Koch, showed that the disease could be induced deliberately by means of these micro-organisms. Pasteur was able not only to confirm this but also proved that the infection could be passed on to sheep kept in fields where animals lay buried which had died of the disease. This is due to the fact that earthworms carry the spores of the *anthrax* bacterium to the surface.

Pasteur decided to treat the disease by a new method: vaccination. On 2 May 1881 he went to Pouilly-le-Fort, a farm near Melun, to take up a challenge which had been put to him. Fifty sheep had been placed at his disposal by the Melun Agricultural Society. He vaccinated twenty-five of them with a small dose of *anthrax* and followed this up with a stronger dose twelve days later. On 31 May, the fifty sheep were injected with a lethal dose of anthrax. On 2 June, the twenty-five sheep which had been vaccinated were in perfect health while the other twenty-five had by then died. The efficacy of

Pasteur's method was thus proved beyond doubt.

*   *   *

The most fearful disease which can be transmitted to man by domestic animals is rabies; this, too, was vanquished by Pasteur.

In antiquity rabies seems to have been fairly rare, though Aristotle did mention it, while Celsius, a Roman physician of the first century A.D., gave the first accurate description of the disease. He advised the application of cupping glasses to remove the microbe from the wound. This method remained in use until Pasteur arrived on the scene.

Special legislation was passed at an early stage to deal with the disease. As long ago as A.D. 490 Clovis I, King of the Franks, issued the following regulation:

> If a dog be killed, no indemnity shall be due to its owner in the event of the animal suffering from rabies. In case the owner denies this, he who has killed the animal shall be required to prove that he has seen the said dog attack other animals or humans and has seen it bite its own tongue.

According to an English manuscript of the eleventh century, the correct procedure in the event of a person being bitten by a dog is to cut the 'worm'—i.e. the *fraenum* or bridle on the underside of the tongue . . . It was not until the end of the seventeenth century that an accurate description of the symptoms of rabies was given by Boerhaave, a Dutch scientist.

In the nineteenth century research into the nature of rabies was intensified. At the cost of experiments with dogs (and it is only right to acknowledge that in this instance not only man but dogs, too, stood to gain) Pasteur succeeded in transmitting the disease. Subsequently, he extracted a vaccine from the experimental animals which he had inoculated with rabies, and this enabled other dogs to be immunised.

Finally, Pasteur decided to experiment with humans. His chance came when a young man from Alsace, Joseph Meister, was bitten by a dog suffering from rabies. Pasteur vaccinated Meister and thus saved his life.

* * *

The fact that man and his domestic animals live in close proximity has undoubtedly encouraged the development of veterinary science, which was first practised in Egypt and Mesopotamia, where its beginnings were recorded in the Code of Hammurabi.

The Greek veterinary surgeons (or *hippiatroi*) and their Roman colleagues accurately described the various animal diseases, although the treatments they recommended were, of course, of limited value. It was the Arabs who first raised the veterinary treatment of horses to a genuinely high level.

In the Middle Ages, veterinary medicine was still regarded as a manual trade, of a half empirical and half religious nature, consisting, above all, of prayer and incantation. Its practitioners were known as 'farriers'. In 1598, an *Anatomia del Cavallo* (Anatomy of the Horse) appeared in Bologna. This work was long believed to be by C. Ruini, but is now thought to have been written by that universal genius, Leonardo da Vinci.

In 1762, C. Bourgelat, the author of the first *Book of the Horse*, also established the world's first school of veterinary medicine in Lyons. In 1766, a similar school was set up at Maisons-Alfort and this was followed in 1828 by yet another in Toulouse. Since then the science has never looked back.

[1] Trials on charges of bestiality should also be mentioned in this context: the person and the animal accused were put to death together, sometimes without proof, upon simple denunciation.

[2] Editions Maisonneuve, Paris 1969.

CHAPTER FOURTEEN

Some Strange Products

ONE OF the most welcome qualities of
domestic animals—as we have noted—is that they provide man with
a range of common consumer goods: meat, eggs, hides, wool, honey,
etc.

A number of species, however, furnish more exotic products, and it
might be interesting to review these briefly. Thus, in the distant past
the Mexican Indians used to rear the cochineal beetle in order to
produce a dye. Let us recall that these are small insects of the order
Homoptera which suck the sap of their host plants; the female is
protected by a waxy 'shield'.

The Indians bred two species: the wood and, above all, the *nopal*
cochineal beetle. The latter was reared on a type of cactus which is
consequently also known as the 'cochineal cactus'. The Indians would
dip these insects into boiling water and then dry and grind them to a
powder, which was dissolved in a solution of sodium carbonate and
alum. The product thus obtained was known as carminated lacquer, a

red dye used to colour fabrics, sweets and other goods. The dye was widely used in many parts of the world including Europe. In 1580, a Spanish fleet brought 70 kg of cochineal powder from Mexico, and in 1887 France imported 399 kg of cochineal and cochineal dye. The practice of rearing these insects spread from Mexico to the Caribbean, the Canary Islands, Algeria, Spain, Corsica and other countries, and the art has long been practised in Persia and India. The cochineal beetle was also used by man as a producer of varnish, for in boring through the bark of fig trees it secretes gum lacquer.

Another remarkable material is bezoar—a hardened mass found in the digestive tract of various ruminants, especially the goats of Iran. The word comes from the Persian *bedzahr*, which means antidote. The substance is believed to cure epilepsy, the pest, fainting, poisoning, etc.[1] It is in fact a round *calculus* or stone of concentric layers enveloping a central nucleus. It consists of insoluble substances secreted in the intestines of the animal and is found not only in goats but also in the digestive tracts of antelopes, llamas and the vicuna. A consignment of llama bezoar was among the treasure lost when a Spanish fleet was wrecked off Cuba in 1628. Bezoar is also produced by some monkeys and the porcupine, and at one time quacks tried to make people believe that there is such a thing as toad bezoar . . .

Bezoar remained in great demand from the sixteenth to the eighteenth century, so much so that it was worth ten times its weight in gold! Eventually, suspicions arose, and one Ambroise Paré therefore decided to carry out an experiment which, though of doubtful morality, cleared up the matter once and for all. He administered poison to a man under sentence of death and then gave him some bezoar to take. The man died, whereupon the King ordered the supposed panacea to be burned.

There is a striking similarity between bezoar and another substance, the famous ambergris, which is occasionally found floating on the surface of the sea: it consists of a hardened mass of intestinal matter found in the body of the Cachalot whale; the latter voids it either through the mouth or the anus. These concretions are formed around remnants of squid—the main ingredient of the cachalot's diet. Greatly prized by the perfumery industry, ambergris has been called 'floating gold'.

The makers of scents also use another substance of animal origin—musk. Various animals possess glands in the anal region from which they secrete a malodorous, greasy liquid, which they use both to drive off their enemies and to mark out the boundaries of their 'territory'.

Two small beasts of prey, the civet and the genet, produce this much-sought-after substance. Most of the civet musk used by the perfumery industry comes from Ethiopia. Occasionally, the same animal is kept for years to be 'milked' for musk. The substance is first collected in hollow cow horns before being refined. Its purpose is to fix other scents, and it is literally worth its weight in gold.

In addition to these carnivores, a small Asian ruminant—the musk deer—which resembles the roebuck and whose canine teeth have evolved, in the male, into a defensive weapon, secretes this precious substance. Unfortunately, to draw the musk, the animal must be killed. The badger secretes a similar substance, known as *castoreum*, which was once considered a magic universal panacea.

Molluscs provide the raw material for a whole range of products, some of which we have already mentioned. Mother-of-pearl, or nacre, a substance highly prized for its iridescent sheen, forms the inner layer of seashells. It is deposited on the 'mantle', a fold of skin from which the substance that forms the shell proper is secreted. Mother-of-pearl is a compound of organic substances collectively known as *conchiolin*, and is deposited continuously around any particles of lime that may be present. A grain of sand, or any other foreign body which has entered a mollusc will be enfolded in a layer of nacre: this is how pearls are formed. Pearls were much valued by the ancient Jews, Greeks, Romans and Arabs. In France, they were first mentioned in edicts issued by Philip IV (the Fair), but their use did not become widespread until the sixteenth century under the reign of Henry II.

At that time the Dukes of Lorraine owned the fishing rights in the Vologne, a small river in the Vosges mountains where fresh-water mussels of a kind which produce pearls are found. It is these pearls which were used by the French royal family, and the Empress Josephine wanted to introduce these mussels in the grounds of the Château de Malmaison. Fresh-water pearls adorned her crown.

The fame of certain individual pearls has survived to this day. Thus, the 'Perigrina' of King Philip II of Spain is known to have been the size of a pigeon egg, and the 'Pearl of Asia', which weighs 121 g, is even larger . . . The pearl oyster, or *Meleagrina*, is, as we have said, the main source both of mother-of-pearl and of pearls. Other molluscs—none of them 'cultured'—such as the fan mussel, the ear shell and the nautilus are also prized for the same reason.[2]

In conclusion, let us mention two other products furnished by molluscs. Bivalves stick to rocks thanks to a tuft of filaments secreted by a gland at the base of the 'foot'. These threads are known as *byssus*. In Sicily and Calabria they are woven into a kind of silk remarkable for its greenish sheen. It is made into cloth, stockings and gloves. Lastly, everybody knows the importance of purple in antiquity. The dye which was used to obtain this colour is secreted by two gastropods, the *Purpurea* and the *Murex*. The Phoenicians set up factories along their coast to process this substance.

[1] See an article by R. Tercafs, 'Le bizarre bézoard', *Découvrir les Animaux*, No. 103, p. 4, 22 March 1972.

[2] In addition to molluscs, other creatures play an indirect part in the formation of pearls: they are two types of fish, the herring and the ablet, which secrete a substance used in the production of cultured pearls.

CHAPTER FIFTEEN

Return to Freedom

WITH THE passing of time, domestic animals belonging to a great many species have reverted to the wild state. We have already mentioned in this context cattle, horses, camels, sheep, goats, etc. Such animals, usually referred to as 'ferals', are particularly numerous on islands in the Pacific and Indian Oceans.

In the Galapagos group, goats which have reverted to the wild state are now present in such numbers as to constitute a plague; they feed on the same plants as the giant turtle and have therefore become dangerous rivals to it. It was on the island of Juan Fernandez, off the Chilean coast, that the real Robinson Crusoe—a seaman by the name of Alexander Selkirk who had been cast adrift by his captain—also found goats which had reverted to the wild state.

Another animal which has regained its freedom has created something of a stir in France. In 1966, four pairs of reindeer were brought to the winter sports resort of Avoriaz in the Savoie Department, the idea being that they should pull sleighs. From a commercial point of view, it was a highly original move, but unfortunately some of the animals fell ill as a result of over-feeding. It was therefore decided to let the remainder run loose during the summer. However, when the time came to recapture the reindeer, they were nowhere to be found, for they had wandered off across the Swiss frontier. When their owners from Avoriaz eventually caught up with them, the reindeer had grown in number, for six fawns had been born in the meantime. Ever since, Savoy reindeer have been roaming the countryside, and their herd is known to have grown further.

Cats and dogs also occasionally revert to the wild state. When this occurs, such animals tend to be regarded as a nuisance. In Asia, for example, dogs of this kind, which roam the streets, are known as 'pariah dogs'. In Europe, they adopt the way of life of beasts of prey, wandering over fields and forests in search of rabbits and young hares, or even the odd nesting partridge. They are skilled in spotting sets and digging up baby hares.

Cats which have returned to a life in the wild lead a similar existence. Such animals must not be confused, however, with the true wild-cat, with which they seem to cross-breed. Many domestic cats, and certainly the so-called 'alley cats', live in a state of semi-freedom, mating at random as they range their area.

This half-way stage between total domesticity and total freedom is interesting from the point of view of genetics, particularly as reflected in the animals' colouring. Many researchers in all parts of the world, including M. Philippe Dreux, of the Zoological Department of the *Ecole normale supérieure* in Paris, have studied this problem.

To obtain data on the colouring of the alley cat, they have used several methods. One is to examine cats in animal shelters and veterinary clinics, but the best technique is undoubtedly to note down the colouring of all cats as and when encountered. Since cats never wander far afield, there is little danger of counting the same animal twice over.

The first results of this study are now known, and they are most interesting. Cats with dark coats are more frequent in the city than in the country: this has been established through a comparative study of cats seen in Paris and in the Mayenne Department. It would therefore seem that an urban environment favours—and enforces through natural selection—the perpetuation of cats with dark coats. The same phenomenon has been observed in London and Marseilles, as well as in Chamonix, a relatively small town, though the preponderance of dark cats is less marked there.

The colour of a cat's coat depends on roughly a dozen different genes, (these, as we have noted, are particles contained within the chromosome; it is through them that the characteristics of living beings are transmitted). In The Hague, unlike Paris, 'marmalade' cats are common, while they are even more numerous in Japan and on the U.S. West Coast. This is due to the predominance of male cats among animals with this colouring, for the gene which controls the colour of a cat's coat is sex-linked.

In Singapore, tabby cats predominate, and in fact account for three-quarters of the feline population. In the Kerguelen Islands, where cats have been introduced by man, nearly all are black, with the occasional black-and-white.

*   *   *

There is another denizen of our cities which has reverted to the wild state and has attained even larger numbers—the pigeon. In fact, a small number of pigeons in our cities—the white-collared dove and the stock dove—are true wild pigeons. The great mass of our urban pigeons are descended from domestic birds which have reverted to the wild state.

This process can be observed in the countryside, where one can occasionally glimpse a flock of pigeons who have strayed from their cote as they regroup in a church steeple. Our cities have gradually become crowded with such pigeons, which have no particular name but are called after the city where they have made their home—*pigeon de Paris*, for example, or 'London pigeon'.

Most famous of all are undoubtedly the pigeons of Venice, where they have become a popular attraction in St. Mark's Square. Each day, as the bells of the Clock Tower strike two, the birds flock to the Square. The office staff of an insurance company are, by virtue of a long-standing tradition, responsible for feeding the pigeons and it is at this hour that the staff appear. The birds are said to have been brought to Venice in the first place by Doge Enrico Dandolo, in 1204. Today, the pigeon population may be as high as 100,000, but recently it was decided that steps must be taken to reduce it.

Paris, too, has a large pigeon population. Exactly where these pigeons have come from is hard to say. Some people believe that the birds' forebears escaped from the pigeon shoot in the Bois de Boulogne, others that the pigeon population of France's capital city was swelled by birds which during the last war took refuge there from the heavily bombed areas of France. There can be little doubt that the pigeon population of Paris also owes something to birds which have escaped from farms and dovecotes. The total number of pigeons in Paris, according to unconfirmed estimates, is about 80,000. Attempts to reduce this total have failed: pigeons caught in nets and later released in the country return to Paris as fast as their wings can carry them.

In the capital, the pigeons nest in every nook and cranny they can find, but never in trees, which they use exclusively as a resting place. Houses they treat as artificial rocks; in fact, their mode of life does not differ all that much from that of their ancestor, the rock-dove, though their reproductive cycle is greatly affected by the urban environment. Their young will hatch and grow up successfully during the most severe cold spells. The twenty-four hour life cycle of the Paris pigeon has been turned upside down, for one can see the birds bustling about in the light of street lamps long after sunset. Since they have no enemies, their numbers have grown unchecked, and their total has not been reduced by a disease known to have afflicted them on a massive scale. They also seem to be very resistant to atmospheric pollution, and can be seen pecking on station platforms within a stone's throw of smoke-belching locomotives. Their food includes grass, berries, tree blossom, bread, grain, etc.

Their plumage is extremely varied: in addition to the traditional grey, one can see black, white, reddish-brown and other liveries, along with countless permutations of colours resulting from the presence of white patches in their plumage or other anomalies. One only has to catch sight of the 'living tapestry' of pigeons thronging the pavements of Paris to become aware of the extraordinary variety of their plumage. Some of these pigeons, in fact, resemble seagulls or crows more closely than their ancestor, the wild rock-dove. One can also see the odd crested and feather-legged pigeon.

CHAPTER SIXTEEN

And Tomorrow?

MAN'S MOST outstanding achievements in domesticating animals date from antiquity. During the last few centuries he appears to have taken no interest in mastering additional species, but now, in this twentieth century of ours, when the machine is king, he has once again turned to the animal world in the hope of discovering new species to harness to his service. A new page has thus been turned in the history of domestication. Animals of many kinds are in process of being domesticated—mammals as well as fish and insects.

The first of these includes the species which offers the greatest promise—the dolphin. Alas, some of the tasks for which people are trying to train this attractive cetacean are, as we shall see, decidedly controversial.

What has happened in our own age is, in fact, merely a rediscovery: way back in the distant past the ancient Greeks regarded the dolphin as man's friend since it will never attack a human being.

According to legend, the poet and musician Arion, having been thrown into the sea by pirates, was picked up by a dolphin which allowed him to ride on its back and put him ashore. Dolphins of a rare species are depicted in a fresco in the Queen's Palace in Knossos, Crete.

Few people know that cetaceans were kept in captivity as long ago as the Middle Ages. The Duchess Marguerite of Flanders owned a porpoise which, round about the year 1400, was kept in a pool in the garden of the palace of the Dukes of Burgundy in Dijon. The porpoise, which had doubtless been caught in the North Sea, had been presented to the Duchess by her husband.

In March 1417, Charles VI of France gave a porpoise to his wife Isabeau of Bavaria. This animal had been caught off the coast of Normandy and was kept in a pool at the Hôtel Saint-Pol, in the Marais district of Paris. Some time after that, Charles VII and Mary of Anjou included a porpoise in the collection of animals they kept in the grounds of the Château de Chignon; it had been presented to them by the Bailiff of Evreux. Nothing is known of the method used at that time to transport these animals . . . From the end of the nineteenth century onwards, larger cetaceans were brought to Europe from America by steamer.

At about that time, people began to realise that dolphins could be of great service to man. For instance, from 1887 to 1912 a dolphin known as Polorus Jack guided ships across the perilous Cook Strait in New Zealand.

It was not, however, until the twentieth century that people began to study the animal scientifically. An American biologist, J. C. Lilly, was the first to realise the dolphin's remarkable potential. Since it does not see well and has no sense of smell, its hearing plays a dominant part in its life. While the dolphin has no vocal chords, its larynx—the passage which gives access to the respiratory tract—vibrates: it produces a whole range of sounds, some of which are audible to man while others are not. These sounds are emitted through the dolphin's nostrils or blow-holes, and not the mouth.

The audible sounds the dolphin makes are whistling, clacking, clicking, and gnashing noises; the inaudible ones are ultrasonic vibrations which the dolphin uses to locate both its prey and any obstacles. The time it takes a sound from the moment of emission to the moment it has been bounced back after striking an object indicates the latter's location. This process is called echo-sounding or *sonar*, and is also used by other animals, e.g. the bat.

The dolphin also uses the noises it emits as a means of communication. Lilly gradually succeeded in communicating with dolphins: when he held out his hand towards them, they approached, clicking their jaws. Once they had got used to the sound of the human voice, they began to imitate it and to make noises, both in the water and out of it, which vaguely resembled human speech. Lilly's dolphins at first made half cackling half prattling noises; later they took to wailing not unlike a baby, until eventually they succeeded in imitating human laughter and song, and even in articulating a few words, such as 'three, two, three'.

The language of the dolphin is one of the most complex in the animal kingdom and is still being studied by many scientists. All are agreed that the dolphin is among the most intelligent of animals, and ranks in this regard with the social insects, certain birds and the primates. However, the evolution of the dolphin has been hindered by its lack of prehensile organs comparable to our hands. Its flippers do not enable it to grasp objects and hence, despite its advanced brain, the dolphin's potential is limited.

But even though it lacks hands, the dolphin is capable of acquiring amazing skills. This has by now become a familiar fact, for the dolphin is a star of the circus and music hall. In Paris, for instance, magnificent displays of dolphin skills can be seen in the *Jardin d'acclimatation*. Leaping high out of the water, the dolphins in the *Jardin*, with their noses, touch a ball suspended several metres above the surface. They also play basket ball, catch rings and slip them over their noses and pull a small boat with a child in it. Between acts, they relax by performing frantic leaps.

Dolphins like to stand upright in the water, their bodies protruding out of it, and they remain in this position for seconds on end. They can even clamber out of their pools. The latter must be kept filled with clean water and be fairly large. Unfortunately, one occasionally sees dolphins kept in pools which are too small. They need plenty of food: about 8 kg of fish a day.

In the 1914–18 war, an American physicist, Robert Wood, put forward the idea of using dolphins for military purposes or, to be more exact, for locating German submarines. Experiments conducted in 1917 by the British Admiralty showed that the animals are in fact

sensitive to the sound of propellers and can be trained to give warning
of such sounds.

Later, the possibility was considered of making dolphins carry
explosives with a view to destroying hostile ships. Another possibility
that was discussed was the use of dolphins to locate torpedoes, mines,
enemy divers, etc. The Americans are said to have used dolphins in
the Vietnam war.

A dolphin which went by the name of Taffy proved that those who
had credited his kind with a great potential were quite right. Taffy
took part in the American Sea-Lab II under-water expedition. His
job was to fetch and carry tools and measuring instruments, to keep
an eye on the safety of divers and to guide any of them back who
might have strayed too far from the ship.

Taffy was subsequently attached to a missile launching base: his
task was to recover the electronic equipment of missiles which had
plunged into the sea. Taffy was trained to home on these devices
using the audio signal they put out as a beacon.

Not surprisingly, the use of dolphins for this type of work gave rise
to some misgivings. On the other hand, it should be remembered that
dolphins have also been employed on purely peaceful tasks, e.g. as
beach guards on the Basque coast.

Of late, dolphins have been used on a mission which is by no means
without danger: their task is to protect bathers from attack by sharks.
The dolphins are taught to patrol a specific stretch of coast: as soon as
one of them has sighted a shark it presses a button that activates a
device which releases more dolphins into the sea so that they can join
in the chase. They either pounce on the shark and kill it, or lure it into
a trap.

Professor René-Guy Busnel, an expert in animal communication,
has recently published a report on his discoveries on the Mauritanian
coast.[1]

He says that each day at dawn, the fishermen there check the colour
of the sea: any change indicates the approach of a shoal of mullet. As
soon as the shoal has been sighted, one of the men enters the water,
beating it vigorously with a stick.

Within minutes, fins invariably loom up off shore: dolphins! They
usually come in packs of about ten. Meanwhile, the fishermen cast
their nets, so that the mullet are cornered between the dolphins on
one side and the fishermen on the other. In a vain bid to escape from

this trap, they leap into the air. Fishermen and dolphins thus co-operate in what can only be called team-work fishing. As soon as they both have caught enough fish—a process which generally takes twenty to thirty minutes—they stop. The dolphins involved belong to a number of species, notably the rare *Souza teuszi*.

Such an association, a true symbiosis between man and dolphin, is truly extraordinary. It is remarkable how these cetaceans respond to the sound signal made by the fishermen, and equally interesting is their easy familiarity: they are not afraid to swim quite close to humans.

This association between man and dolphin was in fact first described a very long time ago: Pliny the Elder devoted an entire page of his Natural History to it. People would not believe him, however, convinced that he was 'shooting a line'. And yet, Pliny's account tallies in every respect with Busnel's observations. The only difference is that the Roman naturalist was describing the observa-tions he had made along the coast of the Languedoc region.

The link between fisherman and dolphin reminds one of the pre-historic cooperation between hunter and dog and is thus of particular interest within the context we have been discussing in this work. It would be difficult to find other such examples in our own time, although it is said that in Australia killer whales have in the past co-operated with whalers in catching whales.

One association which is well known, however, is that between the indicator bird or honey-guide, and man. This is an African bird which guides man (and even more frequently, a carnivore, the ratel or honey-badger) to the nests of wild bees. The indicator is very fond of wax, but is unable to split open the bees' nests. A man or a honey-loving animal therefore has to perform this task for it, and this is the only way it can get at the wax.

Occasionally, man happens to discover the presence of a bees' nest before the indicator bird, which will in that event appear on the scene later. These two symbioses, man–dolphin and man–indicator bird, are the first stages in two processes of domestication which are taking place before our very eyes.

The dolphin is not the only marine mammal man is thinking of domesticating. The killer whale, a large—and very voracious—black and white cetacean, measuring 5 to 9 metres in length, also appears to be highly intelligent. Specimens are on show in a number

of aquariums. One, owned by the Antibes 'Marineland' and called
Clovis, was brought from the Northern Pacific to the French Riviera
by plane. This was no mean feat since the animal weighed no less
than 12.5 tons.

Man is also showing considerable interest in the sea lion. At a U.S.
Navy base in California sea lions are being trained to locate lost
rockets as well as submarines which have strayed off course. The
animals are kept on a lead and gradually trained to undertake expedi-
tions over increasing distances. Eventually, a clip-like device with a
trailing cable is fixed to the animal's nose. When a sea lion has found a
rocket, the clip automatically attaches itself to the projectile. These
experiments, too, have led to protests from animal-lovers, who do
not like the idea of sea lions being used as *kamikaze* warriors.

*   *   *

Several species of land mammals are also in the process of being
domesticated. The most important of these is the eland (*Taurotragus
oryx*). The eland is a powerful African antelope, 1.60 metres high at
the shoulder, and weighing up to 900 kg. Its coat is fawn with white
spots, and it has upright spiral-shaped horns.

If this species could be domesticated, this would be of great benefit
to Africans since it is not a carrier of sleeping sickness and, moreover,
its milk is highly nutritious. Experiments being made with the eland
in the southern Ukraine in the Askaniya-Nova National Park, where
local 'cowboys' look after herds of eland in the steppes, appear very
promising.[2] In the evening the females are milked just as if they were
cows. The average yield is 600 litres a year; the fat content is 14 per
cent, while the protein value of eland milk is double that of cow's
milk. There are also indications that eland milk is helpful in the treatment of certain diseases of the skin and the digestive system.

More than the eland itself, it is the offspring of crosses between it
and cattle which may in fact have the greatest economic potential. At
Askaniya-Nova the Russians have succeeded in crossing male elands
with cows.

In South and East Africa, research has been done into the economic
potential of Thomson's and Grant's gazelles, as well as of the impala
and the springbok. The Highveld Agricultural Research Institute in
South Africa, after testing the meat of the blesbok, the eland, the
gemsbok, the impala, the springbok and the Black wildebeest, came

to the conclusion that the meat of the springbok surpasses all the others in quality.

Other antelopes, too, have been reared on farms, but in these cases the aim was to ensure the preservation of the species concerned. This applies, in particular, to the *bontebok* and the *blesbok*, two breeds of the species *Damaliscus dorcas*, or damalisk.

It would undoubtedly be beneficial from the ecological point of view if it were possible to rear certain African antelope species, for even in the wild state their herds do less damage by erosion than herds of cattle and goats. It is ironical that sixty centuries after the Egyptians had succeeded in doing so, modern man is again trying to domesticate these animals!

Promising results have also been achieved with other ruminants. One such is the elk—a tall Nordic deer with palmate antlers. People have repeatedly tried to domesticate the elk, impressed, above all, by its great endurance and speed. Prehistoric paintings have been found in Russia showing elks harnessed to carts. The elk is said to have been used in Sweden in the seventeenth century to pull mail coaches, and according to some accounts, the Yakut tribe in Siberia used the elk as recently as the last century. Up to now people have probably bred the animal mainly for its milk.

Serious attempts to breed the elk have been made in recent times in Finland and the U.S.S.R. In 1938, an experimental centre at Serpukhovsk, near Moscow, had thirteen tame elks, capable of pulling sleighs over distances of up to 80 km. Later, in 1946, an elk farm was set up in Siberia. There, the baby elks are first hand-reared and then accustomed to a lead. They can be trained to carry loads of up to 250 kg and to pull maximum gross loads of 1,800 kg.

In America's Great North, a start has recently been made with breeding the musk ox. Its thick, shaggy coat furnishes wool of unsurpassed quality. Another species, first domesticated a long time ago, also seems to have a considerable economic potential: the dromedary. In view of the fact that there were camels in North America in the Quaternary era, Dr. Paul S. Martin, of the University of Arizona, believes that the dromedary could be successfully reintroduced on a large scale: the semi-desert regions of the U.S. South should suit the animal very well.

A number of carnivores are also being domesticated. In Australia, experiments are being made to turn the dingo into a sheep dog; the results so far seem promising. The dingo, a member of the dog family, with a dun coat, occurs only in Australia; its origin remains a mystery. Some people believe it to have been introduced from Asia by the first humans to settle in Australia. At all events, the aborigines like to catch their dingos young; they rear them with great care and use them as game dogs. The dingos, however, leave their masters as soon as they become aware of the urge to procreate, and never come back.

We have already spoken of the fox in discussing the breeding of animals for fur. Considerable progress has been made in domesticating a number of strains. The offspring of 'tame' foxes are themselves docile, and what might be called 'domestic' foxes have been reared after several generations of breeding from captive stock. Their temperament resembles that of a dog, and they are very fond of playing with their masters.

Another carnivore which might yet become a popular pet is the leopard. However, as we have said, this is no animal to be left to the whims of all and sundry. In this respect, it resembles the dolphin: genuine domestication, yes; eccentric treatment, no![3]

In our review of domesticated animals, there is one notable gap: the monkey. Although it is the animal most closely related to man, it has always resisted attempts to domesticate it. There are, however, indications that some progress has at last been made in this respect. In Malaya, for example, macaque monkeys have been trained to pick coconuts.

Even more remarkable are the skills of a certain shepherd who lives in the Windhoek area of South West Africa (Namibia) and each morning takes a herd of goats out to graze and brings it back to the farm in the evening. The amazing thing is that the shepherd is in fact a female baboon.

At first, it was the goats which led the baboon, but now it is the other way round. Ahla, the baboon, knows each of the eighty goats of 'her' herd individually. She takes up her position on a tree—or if there is none handy she climbs on the back of the biggest goat—and thus keeps an eye on the herd. Any goat which strays from the herd has Ahla to reckon with: she very quickly sees to it that the goat rejoins the rest.

In the evening, back in the kraal, the baboon makes sure that all is well with the kids. If a female should call for her offspring, Ahla will

find it and take it to its mother. Every now and again the farmer tries
to take a kid from a goat which has too many young and to give it to
one which has none. But Ahla will have none of this: she invariably
gets hold of the kid and takes it back to its natural mother. In the last
century, another baboon, called Jack, is known to have worked on
the railways: he could work the signals and knew how to operate a
small rail cart.

*   *   *

A relation of the bee, the bumble-bee, has been reared for utilitarian
ends and may soon become truly domesticated. We know that this
attractive insect plays an important part in the pollination of flowers:
in searching for nectar in the heart of the flower, the bumble-bee
invariably picks up a few grains of pollen which it later deposits——
quite automatically, of course—on the female organs of reproduction
of another flower.

There are plants which cannot be fertilised without the bumble-
bee. This is true, for example, of lucerne and red clover. Farmers have
therefore considered rearing the insects in order to step up production
of these crops. This policy has in fact been followed in New Zealand,
where in the ninetenth century, clover production was declining
before the bumble-bee was introduced. In Canada, what might be
called the 'domestication' of the bumble-bee is now in progress.

It so happens that the bumble-bee is easy to rear. Children know
this and, in Europe, have practised this art for a long time. The strain
of bumble-bee which is most suitable is that with a reddish-brown.
abdomen. The insect makes its nest in hollow stones and all one has to
do is to pick up the stone, block up the hole, take the stone home and
put it in the garden. The bumble-bee or bumble-bees will not
abandon the nest.

In Savoy, the children have perfected this technique: they build
'mini-hives' of pinewood and line them with hay. They then place
some bumble-bees which they have previously removed from their
nests by hand or with a fork into the mini-hives together with their
cocoons. At first, they leave the roof off to encourage other bumble-
bees to make their way to the nest of their own accord. After a while,
the children take the mini-hives home. Once there, the insects refur-
bish their nests and make 'cells' from wax where they store the
delicious honey, which can then be extracted with the aid of a straw.

In Belgium, the children organise long-distance bumble-bee races; the top prize goes to the insect which is the first to return to its nest. Care should, however, be taken to ensure that these amusements do not lead to a reduction in the bumble-bee population.[4]

Fig wasps, or *Blastophaga*, are essential for the pollination of the fig tree. The people of Smyrna therefore grow wild fig trees (in whose branches these insects thrive) side by side with cultivated ones. When the cultivated fig was first introduced into California, the trees bore no fruit whatsoever. Wild figs had to be imported first; the *Blastophaga* they sheltered then took care of the pollination of the cultivated figs.

Nowadays insects are reared, above all, for another reason: to help us in the biological battle against pests. To destroy an insect pest, another insect, which preys on the pest, is used. This technique, which is unfortunately not yet employed on as large a scale as it should be, has great advantages over chemical insecticides. After at first seeming highly promising, it was realized that the use of chemicals greatly upsets the balance of nature. Moreover, insect strains resistant to chemicals have begun to appear. The use of biological techniques, on the other hand, does not cause pollution and affects exclusively the species whose numbers are to be reduced.

It is, of course, necessary that this method of fighting insect pests and other harmful animals should be used under scientific supervision and with restraint. Without this, the results can be disastrous, as happened with the introduction of the mongoose into the West Indies. These carnivores were imported into the islands to reduce the population of venomous snakes. Unfortunately, the voracious little creatures attacked the island's birds and mammals and all but wiped out the larger insectivores. Agricultural experts are now trying to perfect techniques combining biological and chemical methods.

The insects used for this are now being produced in special laboratories. In France, the National Institute of Agriculture Research at Antibes has such an establishment, which specialises in producing ladybirds, for this pretty insect of the order *Coleoptera* is an inveterate enemy of the greenfly and the cochineal beetle.

When the *Icerya purchasi*,[5] a cochineal beetle, invaded Europe from Australia and did severe damage to orchards, the introduction of a ladybird, *Novius cardinalis*, its enemy in Australia, made it possible to wipe out the pest. More recently, thousands of ladybirds reared at the

Antibes Institute have been let loose in Mauritania, where they put an end to the ravages of a cochineal beetle which was threatening to kill the local date palms.

Various species of *Hymenoptera* also play an active part in the war against insect pests. Thus, in the Italian Alps, special 'farms' have been established for the rearing of red ants. It has been estimated that there were one million red ant nests in the region, equivalent to some 300,000 million ants. To feed their larvae, the ants consumed about 14,000 tons of insects a year. The ants reared on the 'farms' are sent by road to other Italian forestry areas.

Wasps of the species *Prospaltella perniciosa* are used to combat the San Jose scab, a fruit tree pest. The wasp lays its eggs among the larvae of the scab. To fight a pest which ravages the olive groves of the Mediterranean, an insect of the order *Hymenoptera, Opius concolor,* is utilised. *Trichogrammidae* are sometimes reared in hundreds of thousands and released to feed on the eggs of harmful insects. Some of these predators now being marketed commercially.

Insects are not alone in being utilised in the biological battle. Both *Acaridae* and snails are sometimes used in the struggle against their own kind. Let us also recall in this context the fish used to destroy mosquito larvae.[6]

*   *   *

Finally, there is aquaculture, i.e. the rearing of fish and other marine animals—the last front on which man is trying to add to the number of species he has managed to master.

To be exact, this is not an entirely new departure. The Romans practised aquaculture, although—as we have noted, there is some question about the accuracy of the reports on their moray fish tanks.

It is Japan which leads the world in aquaculture—which is a difficult field since it is by no means easy to rear sea fish and crustaceans. The exact conditions (temperature, salinity, etc.) to which they are accustomed in their normal habitat must be reproduced in their tanks. Also, they must be properly fed and the producers must bear in mind that many species of fish are herbivorous when young but turn carnivorous later.

In France, the Centre océ anologique de Bretagne has since 1971 been engaged in the rearing of sea bass and turbot. More than 100,000 larvae were hatched from the eggs of eight female turbot, and 20 per cent of these larvae were kept alive for more than twenty days during which they were fed on live prey. Later, unfortunately, all but two of them died. The two survivors covered themselves up with sand, just like adult turbot. The experience of this institute shows how difficult an undertaking fish farming really is. In 1972, a lobster farm was set up on the island of Houat. Tens of thousands of baby lobsters were bred there and later released into the sea to replenish existing stocks. The work done with other species—sea bream, sole, sea trout and, among crustaceans, shrimp—also appears promising.

*   *   *

It could well be that the scope for domesticating animals is even greater. It is indeed by no means impossible that various species which people have never even thought of in this context—or which have until now resisted all attempts to induce them to breed in captivity—may one day yield to man's efforts to domesticate them.

Philippe Janvier, a zoologist on the staff of the Muséum de Paris, has suggested a hypothesis which is nothing if not ingenious and indeed fascinating. He believes that man may one day succeed in putting to use giant squids, which can measure up to 20 metres. Like its relative, the octopus, the squid is an intelligent creature; moreover, its prehensile tentacles give it a high degree of skill—a quality lacking in marine animals. Once trained, these monsters could be used, for example, to help in raising shipwrecks.

For the present, these are only dreams, but dreams, as history shows, often come true.

[1] 'Relation symbiotique entre hommes et dauphins sauvages', *Revue du Palais de la Découverte*, No. 9, June 1973, pp. 15–28.

[2] See article by R. Tercafs, 'Les animaux domestiques de l'an 2000', *Découvrir les Animaux*, No. 70, 14 July 1971.

[3] In April 1973, some gangsters in Lyons had a clever idea: they hid their body under their leopard's bedding.

[4] See R. Pujol, 'Histoire populaire du bourdon', *Sciences*, No. 58–59, pp. 64–9, 1969.

[5] This, incidentally, is one of the rare hermaphrodite insects.

[6] Microbe preparations are also used in the struggle against insect pests, but these agents are not of direct concern to us since they are not, strictly speaking, animal-based.

Epilogue

THE HISTORY of the domestication of animals, from prehistory to the twentieth century, is thus spread out before our eyes as a vast canvas divided into many parts. The domestication of animals is one of the aspects of man's mastery over nature. Unlike other aspects of that mastery, such as hunting, fishing, agriculture and the exploitation of mineral resources, it has not caused irreparable damage.

The question arises whether man is the only animal to have succeeded in domesticating others. The answer, allowing for a tiny handful of exceptions, must be 'Yes', though some animals do in fact manifest behaviour patterns which come close to domestication. This applies above all to the ant. Various ant species raid colonies of weaker ants and capture their larvae and pupae. These captive ants, when fully grown, are forced to feed their 'slave masters' with honey. Occasionally, the 'slaves' do battle in defence of their colony against attacks from other ants. It is rare for the slaves to rebel against their masters, and the penalty for such conduct is death.

The ants' behaviour resembles domestication even more closely in

another respect. Some ants in fact 'rear' greenflies for the sweet fluid
the latter secrete: the greenflies feed on the sap of plants with a high
sugar content. Consequently, the greenflies' excrement is also sweet.
Some ants merely tickle the greenflies with their antennae to make
them disgorge their 'honey-dew'. The worker ants of certain species
take 'herds' of greenfly to plants particularly rich in nectar, while
some ants actually keep their greenfly cooped up in holes in the
ground—what you might call stables for their miniature 'cattle'.

There are no examples known of the domestication of mammals by
mammals other than man, though something near it has been
seen in Africa. In 1969 the zoologist R. L. Eaton observed an
amazing spectacle in Kenya. He watched a pack of leopards tracking
a herd of antelopes. Since the latter were on the alert, the leopards,
despite their great speed, stood no chance of catching any prey. But
suddenly, Eaton saw a jackal racing towards the antelopes. Scared by
the jackals the antelopes never saw the leopards, one of which was
now able to catch up with the herd and to kill an antelope. The jackal
fell upon the remnants of the booty left behind by the feline. This
'team work' technique of hunting, which seems fairly widespread,
benefits both parties involved. There can be no doubt that this is the
way man first succeeded in domesticating the dog, and this too is
how, to this day, the African pygmies hunt.

Man, however, has progressed beyond the stage obtained by the
leopard. In fact, things may well have turned full circle so that one has
to ask oneself whether today his very mastery over certain species of
animals does not sometimes make him their slave. The importance
which nowadays tends to be attached to pets has resulted in some
obvious excesses. Thus, in the United States, ultra-modern luxury
'hotels' for dogs and cats have been set up, where each animal has its
own numbered room with bath *en suite* and equipped with a bed or
litter according to choice. Some of these creatures, we are told, wear
pyjamas at night and the staff tuck them up in their beds. The 'hotel
guests' may also receive mail from their owners, with the staff
having to read their letters to them ... In short, these dogs are
treated as if they were kings, rather like that famous dog King of
Norway.

Have the roles been reversed? The theme of the animal turned
master of man has greatly preoccupied authors since antiquity. In his
comedy *The Birds*, Aristophanes describes an imaginary city founded

by our feathered friends from which even the gods themselves are excluded.

Gulliver, Swift's celebrated hero, after visiting the Lilliputians and the Giants, enters a strange land where horses, the Houyhnhnms, reign supreme and men are treated as Yahoos, the despised slaves of the horses.

The same theme occurs in many twentieth-century books, for instance, Pierre Mac Orlan's *La Bête conquérante*. In his *War with the Newts*, the Czech writer Karel Čapek tells of a threat posed by these amphibians to man's supremacy, while Clifford D. Simak, in his book *Demain les chiens* suggests that 'man's best friend' has taken over as lord and master of the earth.

In his *Planet of the Apes*, which has also been made into a film Pierre Boulle depicts a world where man is dominated by apes more sophisticated than he is himself. Finally, the latest research into the dolphin has inspired Robert Merle's novel *Un animal doué de raison* (An Animal Gifted with Reason).

Regardless, however, of the imaginary happenings described by these authors, man's hold on the world seems firmly assured. This being the case the animals he has domesticated are at least certain not to disappear. They remind us, in our overpopulated world in which wildlife is alas becoming rare, of the heroic epoch when our ancestors succeeded, by patient effort, in taming, conquering and harnessing the most intractable of animals.

Tables

REGIONS OF ORIGIN OF THE PRINCIPAL
DOMESTIC ANIMALS

Europe	Dog
	Bison
	Reindeer
	Pig
	Rabbit
	Goose
	Swan
	Snail
Eurasia	Horse
	Duck
	Bee
Egypt	Cat
	Hyena
	African elephant

	Ass
	Antelope
	Pigeon
Middle East	Cattle
	Goat
	Sheep
	Dromedary
	Wild ass
	Hamster
	Pheasant
North Africa	Ferret
	Canary
Black Africa	Eland
	Guinea-fowl
	Dove
	Ostrich
India	Asian elephant
	Zebu
South-East Asia	Buffalo
	Gayal
	Banteng
	Peacock
Central Asia	Yak
	Camel
	Kiang
Far East	Chinese goose
	Cormorant
	Goldfish
	Silkworm
	Ailanthus moth
North America	Silver fox
	Turkey
South America	Llama
	Alpaca
	Guinea-pig
	Chinchilla
	Muscovy duck
	Cochineal beetle
Australia	Black swan
	Budgerigar

THE BEGINNINGS OF THE DOMESTICATION
OF ANIMALS

Year B.C.	Sahara Niger	Greece	Yugoslavia	Russia	Northern and Central Europe	Middle East
3000						
					Horse	
	Cattle					
4000						
				Cattle Horse		
5000						
			Sheep			
6000						
		Goat				Cattle
			Cattle			Dog
		Cattle				
7000						
		Dog Sheep Pig				Wild ass
				Dog		
8000						
						Goat Sheep
9000						

TIME OF THE APPEARANCE IN EUROPE OF DOMESTIC ANIMALS OF EXOTIC ORIGIN

Prehistory	Goat
	Sheep
Greek Era	Cat
	Cattle
	Domestic fowl
	Guinea-fowl
	Peacock
	Pigeon
	Parakeet
	Goldfish
Roman Era	Ferret
	Ass
	Pheasant
	Dove
	Silkworm
Middle Ages	Leopard
(up to fifteenth century)	Camel
Fifteenth century	Turkey
	Canary
Sixteenth century	Guinea-pig
	Muscovy duck
	Cochineal beetle
Eighteenth century	Jaco (Grey parrot)
Nineteenth century	Black swan
	Budgerigar
	Ailanthus moth
	Nephila spider
Twentieth century	Hamster
	Dolphin

Note the number of American species which appeared in the fifteenth and sixteenth centuries following the discovery of the New World.

Index

The index, which deals with animals rather than Man, treats the word 'Animals' in its widest sense from mammal through to sponge. As far as possible the various species are indexed under the common English name. The group entries such as Ruminants and Fowls are cross-referenced to the individual specie; to avoid complication, the singular form has been adopted as Mouse, not Mice. The user will find the entry under the word 'Animals' a useful guide to other entries which are of a general nature, such as Domestication. The letter-by-letter system of alphabetisation has been adopted throughout.

Compilers: R and R Haig-Brown of Sherborne, Dorset.